Supporting Children and Parents through Family Changes

Edited by
Anne B Smith and Nicola J Taylor

Children's Issues Centre
National Seminar Proceedings
November 1995

University of Otago Press

Published by the University of Otago Press
in association with the
Children's Issues Centre
Manawa Rangahau Tamariki
University of Otago, PO Box 56, Dunedin

First published 1996
© Children's Issues Centre 1996

ISBN 1 877133 07 8

Design by Jenny Cooper
Printed by the University Printery, Dunedin

Contents

Struggle

A man found a cocoon of the emperor moth and took it home to watch it emerge. One day a small opening appeared, and for several hours the moth struggled but couldn't seem to force its body past a certain point.

Deciding something was wrong, the man took scissors and snipped the remaining bit of cocoon. The moth emerged easily, its body large and swollen, the wings small and shrivelled.

He expected that in a few hours the wings would spread out in their natural beauty, but they did not. Instead of developing into a creature free to fly, the moth spent its life dragging around a swollen body and shrivelled wings.

The constricting cocoon and the struggle necessary to pass through the tiny opening are God's way of forcing fluid from the body into the wings. The merciful snip was, in reality, cruel. Sometimes the struggle is exactly what we need.

(Source: Leadership, shared by Quote magazine)

1 Introduction

There are many complex transitions in the lives of children between birth and adulthood; from starting preschool, to making a new friend, learning to read, or to moving house. There can be no transition, however, which has such a profound effect on so many other aspects of children's lives as changes in family structure due to the separation, divorce or remarriage of their parents. Bronfenbrenner (1979) said that the family 'is the most powerful structure known for nurturing and sustaining the capacity of human beings to function effectively in all domains of human activity – intellectual, social, emotional and physiological'. If the family configuration changes, through the breaking or reforming of parental partnerships, then there are stresses and strains on the nurturing capacity of the family. Children can and do survive these disturbances in family functioning. The stresses may be temporary and may be overcome by the presence of a number of factors. There is little value in bemoaning the breakdown of the family or blaming parents. Relationships have always broken down, and there may have been just as much stress for children in families where the parents still lived together but did not have a good relationship. The realities of today's family life are that many children will experience the separation, divorce or remarriage of their parents. There is, however, a great need for policies and practices to be developed within legal, social welfare, psychological and other family support services to help families emerge as positively as possible from such transitions.

This National Seminar was an attempt by the Children's Issues Centre to get beyond vague generalities of 'strengthening and supporting the family' and focus some careful attention and analysis on what we need to know and do to improve the situation for children and families undergoing change. We brought together people who work with families in different capacities to look at the issues. There are no immediate easy solutions to such complex problems. If, however, researchers and professionals can work together in a collaborative relationship, and if policy makers are responsive, then there are ways in which the situation can be improved in New Zealand in practical ways. We cannot just allow these problems to continue without seeking ways to address them if we are a society which cares about its future. As in so many areas relating to children, it is important to provide the support when children are young and vulnerable. Waiting until the problems reach crisis proportions only leads to a generation of unhappy, maladjusted adults who cannot function adequately in relationships.

Many generalisations about the nature of the family in New Zealand today and in the past, have been made in an ignorant and uninformed way. The work of demographers like Ian Pool is essential if we are to act on the basis of reliable and recent information about the New Zealand family. Pool's paper provides an excellent summary of the demographic data about family size and structure, age of reproduction, marriage and divorce rates and resources available to families. Ngapare Hopa uses the metaphor of the torn whariki to talk about the wear and tear caused by many social changes on Maori whanaungatanga. She shows the complexity of the situation for Maori families and describes the diverse reality, understandings and experience of whanau within the Maori world, and the danger of rationalising it apart from the wider Maori (and pakeha) context.

In order to develop better ways of addressing the issues facing families, we need research which shows how marital transitions affect children. There is a massive literature in this area showing that children do not usually emerge unscathed from the experience. My paper attempts to summarise past research and ask which areas need more attention in the future, to provide positive support for families and children and resolve dilemmas.

The family exists within the macrosystem of the wider society. The legal system is one embodiment of society's values and beliefs which has a profound impact on family life, especially in cases of separation and divorce. Judge Blaikie's years of intensive experience working with family breakdown gives him a unique insight into the current problems and how the family court tries to support families and children. Annis Somerville's work as a family lawyer has involved much attention to the economic realities resulting from a family breakup. Mark Henaghan talks about the importance of the child's welfare as a paramount legal consideration, how successful this process has been in previous cases, and the enormous complexities involved in reaching appropriate decisions. The Family Court needs sound advice from psychologists and other professionals who can talk with and understand children and observe the nature of family life to make careful judgements about what is 'in the best interests of the child'. Max Gold's experience with working with children and writing reports for the Family Court has given him the view that we need to develop better ways of attending to children's perspectives and supporting children in responding to family breakdown.

Panel discussions were a very central part of this seminar and not just a sideline. The session where family members spoke of their experiences in the process of family change were profoundly moving for the participants in the seminar. It is very important not to detach ourselves too much from the individual lived experiences of family members. It will not be possible to improve situations for family members without an understanding of the various experiences that they have had. Sarah's story, for example, puts a human face on the generalisations we know from research about the effects of divorce on childre. Professionals who are working at the coal face of family support services are close to the families who are undergoing change. Their varied challenges and strategies in providing the best help and support for families give many positive directions where services can be improved.

This was the first National Seminar for the Children's Issues Centre. We have much more to learn and much more to do. But we feel that this seminar has provided an excellent starting point for our research and education programmes. We will continue to work with other researchers, professionals, parents, and policy makers in any way we can to give national prominence to this issue which affects so many families in so many ways.

ANNE B. SMITH
Director,
Children's Issues Centre
February 1996

Family Demographic Changes: Good News or Bad News?

Ian Pool
Professor of Demography
Director, Population Studies Centre, University of Waikato

Family Demographic Shifts: Popular Views, Moral Panic and Policy

Over the last few years major shifts in family demographic dynamics and structures have come very much under the microscope. This scrutiny has generally produced negative conclusions, at times generating deep expressions of concern and hand-wringing. The net result is widespread fear, which I will call moral panic, leading to prognostications that the family as we know it is finished. This process occurs even among professional social scientists such as the American Brigitta Berger who recently visited New Zealand. Some blame the family's alleged demise for many of society's ills, especially those which are seen to have an adverse effect on children and youth, and others even go as far as to argue that the very foundations of western civilization are being eroded. Not surprisingly, this wave of anxiety has spread into the social and economic policy making process.

This paper must therefore perform two roles. First, it will review what has actually happened, with the aim of setting right the record on the broad demographic parameters underlying the policy issues to be addressed by child development specialists in the rest of this volume. Secondly, this demands that the question be raised whether or not moral panic of the level we are seeing is justified. I am not trying to criticise persons who hold genuine concerns, but if the acute anxieties we hear voiced are not soundly based, it must be asked how and why they have developed, and thus whether they constitute an informed base on which to build policies relating to children's issues.

The argument here is not so much with popular views as with their impact on policy. The nation's social health depends to a degree on sound policies relating to families and their role in child care. In turn, to be sound these policies must be based on a proper stocktaking of the nation's families and the resources available to them. In this respect the publicity generated by the International Year of the Family produced more heat than light on this topic (see Appendix 1).

Finally, by way of introduction, I should note that my paper covers Maori and other ethnic groups, but is focussed primarily on Pakeha families. My colleague, Associate Professor Hopa, in her paper deals with the complex dynamics and structures of whanaungatanga. My paper is also at the macro-level, dealing with populations, whereas hers is much more at the micro-level dealing with dynamics within families.

Antecedents and Issues Shaping Public Discourse on Families

To posit a demise in anything it is necessary to assume that conditions were better in the past. In the family context many commentators, particularly of my generation – I am a baby-boom parent – or Brigitta Berger's, take as their model the stereotypical household of the baby-boom years. We tend to reconstruct it in a somewhat idealised form: a happily married couple in their early to mid-twenties, with two well-adjusted offspring. Somewhat unexpectedly several years later they will conceive a third child, who will become the darling of its older siblings. This baby-boom couple may well have lived in a three bedroom house, say in Te Atatu or Stokes Valley, and there performed their parenting, with mother a leading light in Plunket or the local kindy association, and father away all day as the breadwinner. Of course, such a retrospective picture selectively overlooks the moral panics of yesteryear which produced, inter alia, the Mazengarb Commission of the early baby-boom. This view also fails to recognise that these very same baby-boom couples were the role-models for today's allegedly less adequate parents.

The positing of distinctions between golden eras in the past, and the societal dysfunctions of the present, is a time-honoured privilege of older generations, although, at least in the family domain, it does seem a particularly powerful force at present. Indeed, this contemporary panic is not just a New Zealand phenomenon, but is seen across a number of developed countries. What is interesting, however, is that anxiety appears to be most extreme in what I will call the Anglo-Saxon western countries, notably Great Britain, the United States and New Zealand. It is rather more muted in the western European countries, despite, in some cases, rather more extreme demographic changes. This contrast became clear to me at a meeting I attended earlier this year at Oxford on a major cross-national study on the family and social policy with which a number of New Zealand researchers are involved (12 March, 1995, to discuss an OUP contract to publish the country studies; the New Zealand contribution, co-authored by Peggy Koopman-Boyden, Susan St John, Ian Shirley and the present writer, will be in a volume with Gt Britain, United States and Canada, three of the New Zealand Chapters were primarily written at the Centre, see Johnstone and Pool, under editorial review).

In the Anglo-Saxon countries public discourse runs from sincere and probably well-based anxiety over the effects on families and children of what may be rated as indicators of family dysfunction, notably marital dissolution, through to blaming family changes for most of the economic ills of society. To give an example of this sort of view in Table One I quote the causal analysis and conclusions of the address to the December 1994 Conference of the International Year of the Family, by New Zealand businessman, Alan Gibbs. Moreover, the fiscal malaise of these same countries, and thus calls to demolish the welfare state, is often attributed to family dysfunction, and particularly to the sole-parent unit, which is usually female-headed. Sole parenting is also frequently linked to ex-nuptial and

Table 1: Quotations About Family Policy

I. Decline of the New Zealand Family: Causes

'...for thousands of years societies have said it was fundamentally important to make sure that men did their cultural duty and took responsibility for a woman and her children... We decided we wouldn't bother with men we'd get the state to do it for us. So we swapped husbands for benefits. I don't blame the DPB for the breakdown of marriage.... The DPB followed the social revolution. I think the pill was the most important because it relaxed the pressures that mothers put on daughters to hold this cultural norm together... Most of the problems poor families have today are a result of that huge social change. They have little to do with the state of the economy'.

Alan Gibbs, Panellist 'The Impact of the Changing Economy on Families', *Strengthening Families, Conference International Year of the Family*, 30 Nov - 2 Dec, Auckland. Wellington: IYF

II. Overcoming the Fiscal Consequences of the Family's Demise

'[Social Security Secretary] Lilley Targets Benefits of Lone Mothers',

Heading, *Daily Telegraph*, Mar 31 1995

'(The Personal Responsibility Act) Discourage illegitimacy and teen pregnancy by prohibiting welfare to minor mothers and denying increased Assistance for Dependent Children while on welfare, cut spending for Welfare Programs...'

Contract with America, Rep. Newt Gingrich, Rep. Dick Armery and the House Republicans, Nov 1994

'... where the sole parent has had no relationship in the nature of a marriage with the father of the child, the [DPB] benefit should not be available... we have sent out all the wrong signals about responsibility in personal relations... a young unmarried mother who has not been in an established partnership, under my proposal would be entitled only to the unemployment benefit... a sole parent with children from an earlier marriage or de facto relationship, who had an additional child outside an established relationship, would not be eligible for extra monetary assistance for that child'.

Ruth Richardson, 1995, *Making A Difference*, Christchurch: Shoal Bay Press. pp. 213-14.

III Reallocation of Parenting to Those with Taxable Incomes

'(The Family Reinforcement Act) ...tax incentives for adoption... (The American Dream Restoration Act) A $500 per child tax credit, begin repeal of the marriage tax penalty...'

Contract with America, ibid

adolescent childbearing, two very different phenomena. Table One quotes a heading in the British newspaper, *the Daily Telegraph*, and from the *Republican Contract with America*, both of which specifically target these groups. The slashing of support to dependent children is justified by Republicans in terms of the lack of moral responsibility of the female parents, a theme which also runs through statements of the Hon Ruth Richardson, quoted in the same table.

Underlying these worries, and the genesis of fears about the contribution of the family to the survival of western society, are concerns over declines in fertility to sub-replacement levels. Replacement is achieved in low mortality countries when each woman over her reproductive span has on average around 2.1 children – to replace her and her partner, and to allow for a minimal level of infant and childhood mortality. Here an allied issue is the development of eugenic and potentially racist views, reminiscent of those held in the 1930s and 1940s, that it is the world's poor who are procreating. The fact that Third World fertility is also dropping rapidly is less publicised.

Linked to sub-replacement fertility, but within national populations is another more subtle and potentially divisive factor. The society appears to be splitting into two groups, a minority, typically less well off, who seem to have inherited the capacity the majority appeared to have had in the baby-boom, to conceive with consumate ease at a very young age. Against this today we see the majority who are reproducing at older ages, but among whom are a small minority, often quite affluent, who are involuntarily childless. The occurence of this paradox may lie behind the advocacy of the more punitive measures against teenage childbearing and solo-parenting. To show that this is not an exaggeration I quote the Republican Contract with America (see Table 1), which suggests tax incentives as a means of reallocating the stock of children, and attempts to stimulate more parenting among the middle classes.

In the United States and in New Zealand this paradox has another element to it. It is Blacks, Maori or Pacific Islanders who have higher levels of early childbearing; White or Pakeha, who are the late starters. Yet policy measures taken to restructure welfare often fail to recognise that this demographic difference has severe consequences, as is shown in another paper written with Natalie Jackson (Jackson and Pool, in press).

The Demographic Parameters

The anxieties about decreases in the viability of the post baby-boom family (i.e. since about the early 1970s) seem to fall into two categories, both of which I will review below using vital statistics and census data (the sources and methodologies used here are presented elsewhere in Pool, Davies and Jackson, 1993; Jackson and Pool, 1994 and in press). These two relate to factors endogenous to family demographic changes themselves and constitute the issues I will discuss over most of the rest of this paper:

I   the quantity and perceived quality of reproduction

– the fact that almost all developed western countries are sub-replacement populations;

– the purported increases in cohabitation outside marriage, particularly among the young;

– the increases in ex-nuptial fertility;

– the apparently uneven distribution of fertility by age of mother;

– the separation of the formalisation of unions through a wedding from the process of procreation;

– the role of hormonal contraception in all of this.

II   the quantity and perceived quality of parenting resources

– the decline in the proportion of households which are composed of parents, particularly two-parents;

– the proportion of households composed of sole-parents, particularly those which are female-headed.

At the same time, and to reply to commentators like Alan Gibbs, it is essential to ask about exogenous factors which may have an impact on the family's material capacity to perform its assigned role. This involves shifts in the socio-economic context of these demographic changes (the sources and methodologies used here are described in Johnstone and Pool, under editorial review; Martin, 1995):

Thus, I will look at:

III   the quantity of economic resources available to families.

Finally, I should note that there have been transitions in values systems, but these cannot be detailed here, because, as I have shown elsewhere (Pool, 1992), in New Zealand we can only guess at these by importing findings from overseas. Suffice to say that in Europe and North America representative samples indicate changes between baby-boom and post baby-boom cohorts in terms of the way the actors in families are viewed: from child-centered to seeing the parents needs as also of importance.

This shift has been accompanied by changes from rather more egalitarian community oriented values to New Right neo-liberal attitudes privileging individual freedom. At the same time, the most recent European data suggest an allied increase in conservative political attitudes favouring 'authoritarian... top-down management principles' (Lesthaeghe, 1991; Lesthaeghe and Moors, 1995), but these are not associated with a return to the old style of family. The confused message coming from the New Right raises the question whether it is driven more by fiscal and anti-statist feelings than by genuine concern over the moral status of the family *per se.*

The Quantity and Perceived Quality of Reproduction

The peak Non-Maori baby-boom total fertility rate, represented by data for 1962 in Figure One, constituted an increase to higher levels than at any time since the 1890s, (Pool, 1992; Sceats and Pool, 1985; Jackson and Pool, 1994). In contrast, the Maori rate had remained high throughout the century until then (Pool, 1991). Both rates then decreased at first gradually, and then very rapidly in the 1970s.

The recent accelerated decline is not unique to New Zealand populations. With the exceptions of Iceland and Ireland, over a space of a few years in the 1970s the western developed countries, including North America and Australasia and even the Mediterranean littoral, went through a rapid decline in fertility (Lesthaeghe, 1991), while East Europe has seen the same phenomenon since the fall of communism (Coleman, 1992; Roussel, 1994). The shift to sub-replacement fertility has been so significant in western capitalist countries that it has been termed the 'Second Demographic Transition' (van de Kaa, 1988; for an opposing view see Cliquet,1990). Thus, as is shown in Figure One, a total fertility rate just below two births per woman was reached for Non-Maori around 1980. The New Zealand national figure is very close to the Non-Maori, while the Maori level used to be very different, but has converged with the Pakeha. There is, however, not the same convergence for age-specific patterns (Jackson, Pool & Cheung, 1994).

The decline in Maori fertility in the mid-1970s, as I have shown elsewhere (Pool, 1991), is probably the most rapid on record, even surpassing China's. This fact should be kept in mind as a major demographic context for the family changes Dr Hopa will be discussing in her paper. Furthermore, this rapid demographic transition, or 'shock' to use a term employed by Quebecois demographers (Mathews, 1984), was but one among a number which have had a significant impact on Maori social organisation since World War II. For Pakeha these same changes had been more gradual, spread out over 80 years, and were rather more sequential. For Maori they were radical, over 30 years, and overlapped. Again by way of providing a framework for Dr Hopa's paper, can I note the following additional transitions, which I have detailed in my book *Te Iwi Maori* (Pool, 1991):

- a rapid decline in mortality (1945-61), which had an impact on Maori age structures particularly through improvements in child survival, and decreases in adult female mortality;

- accelerated urbanisation, particularly in 1956-66, often from isolated North Island regions into the major cities;

- a labour-force transformation from the primary sector, which in 1936 was still semi-subsistence in form, to manufacturing and the service industries, then a second brutal transformation into unemployment during the restructuring of the 1980s.

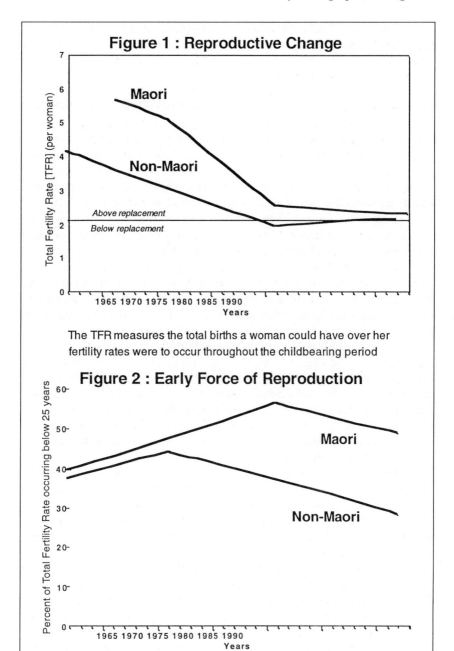

Figure 1 : Reproductive Change

Maori

Non-Maori

Above replacement

Below replacement

The TFR measures the total births a woman could have over her
fertility rates were to occur throughout the childbearing period

Figure 2 : Early Force of Reproduction

Maori

Non-Maori

Since the 1970s, we have seen the demographic manifestations of a rapid Maori family transition. It is important, however, that we do not view this as a phenomenon somehow totally isolated from the other demographic shocks which have preceded or accompanied it.

Returning to the Pakeha family transition, around 1990 a decade after sub-replacement had been reached, a somewhat peculiar trio of countries, New Zealand, Sweden and the United States, with Norway and others trailing a little behind, moved back towards exact replacement. Swedish demographers have attempted to link this blip to welfare statism, particularly family policies favouring parental commitment towards young babies (Hoem, 1990). While I support the principles surrounding parental leave, I do not accept his diagnosis, for the same transition occurred in New Zealand at the period when welfare props were very much under threat. Instead, this reprise was very much a result of demographic causes: the arrival of large cohorts, born in the baby-boom, at the key parenting ages, which by then had shifted up to around 27-35 years.

I have termed this slight reprise a 'baby-blip' to distinguish it from a genuine baby-boom which would have involved much higher total fertility rates, and a major shift back to early childbearing. Around 1990 there was, it is true, a minor but short-lived sub-blip to women at ages below 21 years. The interesting point there, however, is that the adolescent mothers of 1990 had been born at the moment of New Zealand's peak period of teenage fertility, 1970-71. But this sub-blip has proved to be the sole, and insignificant, exception to the major trend in New Zealand as in other western developed countries: a wholesale shift to delayed childbearing. This has had a major impact on every aspect of family life, and is therefore the underlying factor for most of the patterns and trends I am now going on to describe. Moreover, it will be the demographic factor dominating not just family dynamics, but also the nation's economic, fiscal, cultural and social energies into the foreseeable future (IGCPPG, 1990).

Delayed childbirth has had two effects. Obviously, there is a marked decrease in early childbearing, as is shown in Figure Two. Secondly, as is shown in Figure Three, this meant a reallocation, a shift-share across the child-bearing ages of the force of fertility: a movement into the middle and even late period. It should be noted that this is primarily a Pakeha phenomenon, but is also showing up a little in Maori reproductive strategies.

The net result, as is shown in Figure Four, is that Pakeha cohorts have returned to the conservative childbearing of their grandparents; they have rejected the aberrant patterns of the baby-boom. Indeed, this figure shows up the baby-boom parental cohorts, those born fron 1925 to 1954, as very much out of step with previous or more recent generations this century. It is their combination of early and high peak fertility which is so astonishing. Almost one third of all women born 1935-39 had a baby between their 24th and 25th birthday. If one allows for those who had amenorrhaea from a pregnancy prior to their 24th birthday, those who were breastfeeding and less likely to become pregnant, and those who were pregnant but would have a birth after their 25th birthday, this is a very high age-

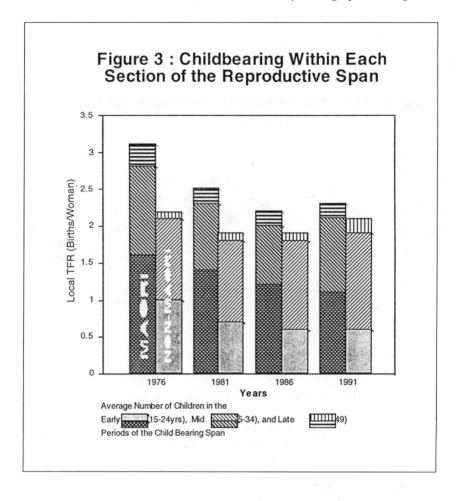

Figure 3 : Childbearing Within Each Section of the Reproductive Span

specific fertility rate. It is a remarkable indication of the powerful effect of the collective norms, and the high degree of conformity of that time.

For Maori the pressures seem even more marked, for almost 40 percent of the cohort of 1940-44 gave birth at their peak age-group of 22 years. In their case this was not a baby-boom but a continuation of previous high levels. For subsequent birth cohorts, the age and level of the peak declined before the peak age started to increase but the level remained low and similar to the Pakahe peak level.

This figure also throws light on another issue. The policy makers of today, say persons aged 35 to 60 years of age, but particularly those born between 1935 and 1950, represent the most deviant parental cohorts this century. Parenthetically, I must add that I am not attacking my own generation, merely locating it in its demographic context. But we must recognise that, whether we are Pakeha or Maori, we bring into the policy debate an historically peculiar set of reproductive

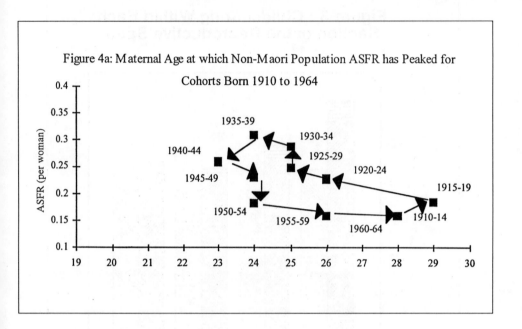

Figure 4a: Maternal Age at which Non-Maori Population ASFR has Peaked for Cohorts Born 1910 to 1964

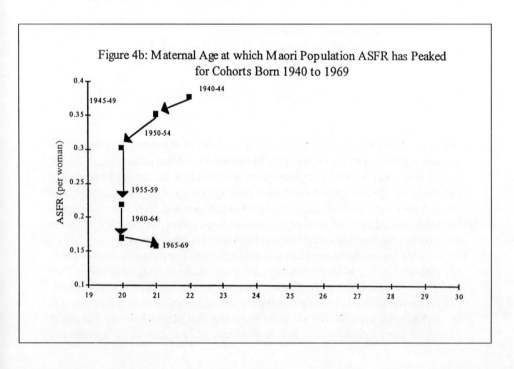

Figure 4b: Maternal Age at which Maori Population ASFR has Peaked for Cohorts Born 1940 to 1969

experiences. Thus we must be particularly cautious about the prognostications and prescriptions we might make. It is the young who are conservative and are following tradition; we rejected it.

This fact shows up above all if one looks at teenage pregnancy. Adolescent fertility has declined very significantly for both Maori and Non-Maori, *in absolute terms as well as relatively* (Table 2). The Pakeha teenager of today pales into insignificance alongside the adolescents of the early 1970s, as can be seen when the comparison is made with the peak year, and for Maori the comparison is with 1962.

Table 2: Adolescent Childbearing		
	Year	
	1976	*1991*
Number of adolescent births	8,666	4,822
Rate per 1,000 adolescents	50	35
Nuptial Rate (per 1,000 married)	396	301
Ex-nuptial (per 1,000 unmarried)	30	32
Proportion of teenage births nuptial	.54	.09
Decrease from Peak Rate:		
Maori: Rate 1991 as % of Rate 1962	60	
Non-Maori: Rate 1991 as % of Rate 1972	42	

This decrease has not been due in any important way to rapid rises in induced abortion rates. From 1981 to 1992, at 11-14 years the abortion rate decreased from an already low 0.7 per 1,000 women at that age, to 0.4. At 15-19 it increased from 12.1 to 16.2 *(Demographic Trends,* 1993; Sceats and Parr, 1995), but was still below levels for Australia, England and Wales, and the United States. It was, however, above that for the Netherlands, whose rate at this age actually declined in this period (Alan Guttmacher Inst., 1990). While known conceptions (births + abortions) increased overall from 1981 to 1991 by 24 per cent (57,573 to 71,461), for adolescents also dropped from 7,408 to 7,147; either teenagers had become less exposed to intercourse than popularly imagined, or had improved their contraceptive techniques. It thus constantly surprises me that in an era when levels of adolescent childbearing are low, and declining except for the mini-blip about 1990, there should be so much public panic about this issue.

The reason is, of course, that teenage reproduction is frequently confounded with ex-nuptial childbearing, data on which are presented in Table 3. Here also a distinction must be made between ex-nuptial conception and ex-nuptial parturition. Declines in adolescent fertility accompanied shifts in the proportion nuptially born, although the absolute number and rate of teenage ex-nuptial births remained

Table 3: Ex-Nuptial Fertility (= EN)			
Year:		*1976*	*1991*
"Local" ENTFR)/woman:	15-19	.15 (42)	.16 (21)
	20-24	.26 (28)	.37 (37)
	25-49	.77 (30)	1.01 (42)
		(100)	(100)
EN Births,25+/Adolescent Births		.27	2.22

Note:
Synthetic "total" rates, calculated as for the Total Fertility Rate.
Thus: "Local" ENTFR, age x = 5 * Sum (ENASFR,x),
where x is age, and ENASFR is the ex-nuptial births to unmarried women.

Figures in parentheses are the percentage distribution by age of the ex-nuptial rate.

almost unchanged. In contrast, in the baby boom a high proportion of all births to women aged less than 21 years had been conceived ex-nuptially, but born nuptially after a precipitated marriage (Pool and Crawford, 1980). The widely publicised increase in ex-nuptial childbearing since then is in part due to a decline in such marriages, but, as Table 3 shows, the most important fact is that ex-nuptial childbearing has shifted to older ages where couples are likely to be in longer-term cohabiting unions. This trend accords with the experience across the developed countries (Reviewed in Pool, 1992).

The upward shift in reproduction has been accompanied, then, by a similar movement in ex-nuptial conception. It has also been associated with a major transformation in patterns in marriage. The most noteworthy aspect to go has been the precipitated white wedding of the baby boom teenage bride, when only the immediate family knew the real truth, although others may have guessed when a mature weight baby was born 'prematurely'. I wish that I could say that everyone lived happily ever after, but as Carmichael (1982) has shown, the highest divorce rates have come from baby-boom marriages at young ages, many of which unions persisted until the 1980s before finally dissolving. In other words, many of the recent trends we have seen in marital breakdown had their origins a long way back in the reproductive patterns of the baby-boom. We must recognise this demographic fact, as it happened to coincide with the changes in divorce legislation – one factor reinforced the other.

A further factor, reported internationally (Santow, 1989), is the separation of procreation and marriage. In the past marriage was preceded or quickly followed by pregnancy; today the reasons for marrying may be linked to a decision to formalise procreation, as the example in Appendix 2 so frankly shows, or may be the result of other factors, such as simple commitment to the other person.

Whatever the reason, two things have happened here and overseas. Registered marriage rates have declined, and, far more importantly, legal marriage is occurring at older ages – it is being repositioned. The number of teenagers who were married in 1991 was 12 percent of the level in 1976, while the decrease for 20-24 year olds was to one third of the 1976 level. In 1971 the mean age for women marrying for the first time was 21.7 years, but by 1991 and 1992 it was back to the figure of the depression year of 1935 of 25.5 years. This repositioning of entry into marriage to more mature ages is reflected in recent increases in first marriage rates at 30-34 years for women.

There are no reliable New Zealand data on cohabitation, but probably we are not too different from Australia. There it is reported that 'the rise in cohabitation also seems to suggest that marriage is not being rejected,... We are brought back to the notion of continuity in the formation of marital unions' (Santow and Bracher, 1994).

Finally, it is important to recognise that we have few data on either the values or the behaviours which have produced these changes. This gap will be partly filled by our Centre's nationwide survey 'Women of New Zealand: Family, Employment and Education', the fieldwork phase of which has just finished in November 1995, on a sample of 3,000 women aged 20-59 years.

The few fragmentary data we have are on mechanisms rather than determinants. Clearly efficient contraception, sterilisation and the hormonal methods play a major role, but operate in a matrix of values, attitudes and knowledge of family planning (Murphy, 1993). The data on abortion are, however, very good and show that, despite recent increases, levels are still relatively low. Sceats and Parr have concluded that increases over the last decade 'reflect two separate phenomena. Firstly, a demographic shift in reproduction to older ages; and secondly the possible impact of social and economic pressures on family formation strategies. It is possible that current trends reflect a short term effect and may already be passing' (Sceats and Parr, 1995).

The Quantity and Perceived Quality of Parenting Resources

The central question for this seminar is an evaluation of family resources. Here there is great deal of concern, fuelled often by incorrect data, and often by a failure to recognise the impact of the upward shifts in marriage and reproduction outlined above.

To show the hazards of analysing household and family data, Table 4 presents data on some commonly used rates. It is clear that even a minor error of the denominator or numerator, or a failure to define terms can produce very different results.

Turning to substantive questions, most importantly there is a decline in the proportion of households which include parents of young children. But this is largely due to a set of demographic 'squeezes' rather than to the decline of the family as a social institution.

Table 4: Conceptual Hazards, Family and Household Data, 1991		
	Pakeha	*Maori*
Parenting FAMILIES, % of all FAMILIES (Fams)	74	87
Parenting FAMILIES, % of all HOUSEHOLDS (H'holds)	41	54
Parenting HOUSEHOLDS, % of all H'holds	46	72
Sole parent FAMILIES, % of all parenting FAMS	22	38
Sole parent H'HOLDS, % of all parenting H'HOLDS	17	29

The general upward movement of the age structure to middle and older ages, produces what is termed demographic momentum, and has a significant impact. The net effect of this momentum was a shift to non-parenting family structures appropriate for various life cycle stages, and not at all suggestive of dysfunction. Between 1976 and 1991, there was a slight decrease, seven percent, in the number of two-parent families, but a massive increase, 51 percent, in non-parenting households.

The effects of this momentum on the Non-Maori population are presented in Table 5. Column one shows the simple demographic effect of changes in the numbers of occupiers of a given age; column two gives the percentage of the change 1976-91 contributed by each age group; and column three shows the proportion of the shifts between categories occurring at given ages. Table 6 identifies for each life cycle stage the main forms of non-parenting which have had such a major impact on shift-shares, particularly at 30-54 years. As I will show below, this is the age at which sole parenting is most important. Nevertheless, the great-

Table 5: The Effects of Demographic Momentum on Growth in the Number and Shift-Shares Between Categories of Households, 1976-91			
Age group Percent change	*Percentage of in number*	*Percentage of momentum effects*	*gross shifts**
15-29	− 3	− 2	20
30-54	+ 26	+ 58	56
55+	+ 27	+ 44	25

Note: * Shifts = Diff. age x between Ob and Ex No.
    Ex(x) = [No. (x, category i, 1976)] X
            [Households (x, 1991)/Households (x, 1976)]
    where, ob = observed, and ex = expected

Table 6: Growth 1976-91, Main Forms of Non-Parenting Households

15-29 Non-related households (eg flatting)
Childless couples
[CAUSE: delayed child-bearing]

30-54 Childless couples in their 30's
[CAUSE: delayed child-bearing]

Empty nester, childless couples, 40-54 years
[CAUSE: parents of the latter part of the baby-boom who
completed heir childbearing at very young ages, and whose
children have left home]

55+ Empty nesters, early baby-boom

Single-person households
[CAUSE: aging, widow(er)hood, but independence]

est contributor to shift-shares at 30 – 54 years, is the impact at both ends of the age group of childless couples. This does not signal dysfunction, but rather that the mid-career family is simultaneously feeling the effects, on the one hand of delayed childbearing among its younger cohorts, and, on the other hand, of early childbearing in the past. This leads to the empty nesting today among its older cohorts, who were the parents of the later baby boom. The squeeze at the upper end of this age-group will soon shift as the late starters of today, currently 25-34 years age themselves, and their children stay in the nest until the parents are in their fifties or sixties. Indeed, it may be reinforced by other factors as, prolonged education, delayed marriage and decreased access to equity may mean that children will stay on even later than that, the 'cluttered nest' syndrome, as Canadians are calling it (Boyd and Pryor, 1989). Together these changes will see a demo-graphically-driven decrease in non-parenting households at this pivotal age.

From a child-issues standpoint the key issue is the family situation of the nation's children. The general conclusion must be fairly positive: most children are in households with two parents, or with two parents and others. Moreover, the changes since the 1970s are less than we might sometimes believe from the media. In 1976, 78 percent of dependent children were in two-parent households, and 94 percent in two-parent or two-parent and others households. By 1991 the levels had dropped marginally to 72 percent and 85 percent. In sum, in 1991 more than four-fifths of our children were in households with two or more adults to care for them.

Table 7 does a more detailed stocktaking, showing that there are variations in this pattern, in particular the role allocated to extended family households. Twenty-five percent of Maori and 35 percent of Pacific Island children are in two-

Table 7: Dependent Children: Percent in Parenting Households						
Occupier	Pakeha		Maori		Pacific Is	
characteristic	1976	1991	1976	1991	1976	1991
A. Percent of total dependent children:						
Ethnicity*	81	73	14	16	2	7
B. Percent of total dependent children of each ethnic group:						
Parental Age						
15-29	17	14	23	30	20	19
30-44	61	73	53	55	61	61
45+	22	13	24	16	19	21
Total	100	100	100	101	100	101
Household type						
2-parent, all	82	79	62	49	52	50
2-par & 2-par+, all	94	87	92	74	95	85
2-par, 15-29	14	9	14	12	10	7
2-par,2-p+,15-29	16	11	20	19	19	14
2-par, 30-44	51	60	36	32	34	34
2-par,2-p+,30-44	58	65	49	42	58	52

* Excludes small number of Asian and Other: 2%, 1976; 4%, 1991

parent plus others units. The table also identifies the effects of the demographic squeeze on Pakeha parenting households; the decreases in the stock of children looked after by young occupiers aged 15-29 years, and older occupiers, as against a significant increase in mid-family life cycle carers at 30-44 years.

Much of the panic over families and many of the more punitive prescriptions are directed at sole parents. It should first be stressed that sole parenting is a situation, into and out of which people move; it is not a permanent status (Pool and Moore, 1986). Secondly, sole parenting is not the same as, nor is it solely determined by, ex-nuptial childbearing. Many sole parents have come through legal divorces, and a fair number are widows. Moreover, sole parents on average care for fewer dependent children than do other parenting households, as is shown in Table 8. Finally, few sole parents are young women living alone. Most commonly, sole parenting is a mid-family life cycle situation.

The confusion over the ages of steretypical sole parents comes from statistics which relate sole parent families to total families by age. At younger ages there are few families formed of any sort, but those that are tend to be sole parent, as is shown in the upper trajectories in Figure 5. The proportion of the female population at those ages in such unions is, however, very small, and is higher from the late twenties until the fifties, as is shown in the lower lines on Figure 5. The lower curves are the better measure of the prevalence and impact of sole parenting.

Table 8: Average Number of Dependent Children 1976 and 1991			
	Pakeha	*Maori*	*Pacific Is*
1976: Female sole parent	1.13	2.17	2.30
Two-parent	1.82	2.63	2.83
1991: Female sole parent	1.02	1.69	1.79
Two-parent	1.46	1.88	2.19

Figure 5:

Female One-Parent Families by Ethnic Group by Age of Mother, 1991

expressed (i) as a Percentage of the Female Population by Age; and
(ii) as a Percentage of Families (One- and two-Parents Combined)
with Occupiers of the Same Age.

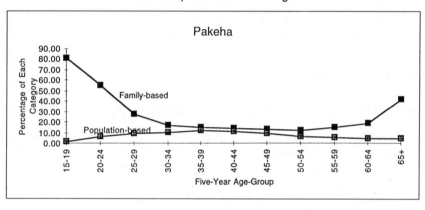

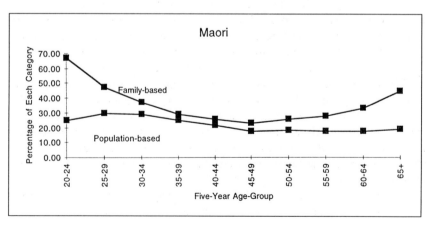

A further confusion arises because of the fact that many sole parents are in two-parent plus others/extended households, where they are not likely to be the social isolate of the stereotypical sole parents. This is illustrated in Figure 6. It shows that sole parent families far exceed independent sole parent households at younger ages for all ethnic groups, and that this continues across the ages for Maori and Pacific islanders.

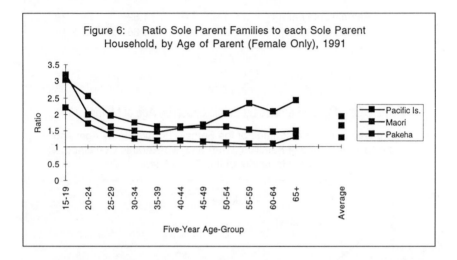

Figure 6:   Ratio Sole Parent Families to each Sole Parent Household, by Age of Parent (Female Only), 1991

The Quantity of Economic Resources Available to Families

This is a very important question worthy of a paper in its own right. To make a reasonable assessment it is necessary to take into account the family labour force participation patterns and family sizes, as well as incomes, adjusted to allow for changes in purchasing power. The Centre has worked on this as part of its contribution to a cross-national study on families and social policy, and the New Zealand paper will be in the first volume which is currently under editorial review for publication by Oxford University Press. I will quote from some of our concluding remarks (Johnstone and Pool, under editorial review; Martin 1995).

Over the last decade or so almost all family categories have suffered real declines in income, with the most severe changes occurring in the latter part of the 1980s. At the beginning of the 1980s two-parent families had been among the higher income group, but by 1991 they were among the lower. This is the single most important family category, and, at the same time is, of course, the stereotypical 'stable' form much favoured by moralists. Thus a decrease in their incomes can hardly be blamed on family changes, and this makes nonsense of Alan Gibbs' attempt to attribute the causes of poverty to changes in family structures rather than on the economy.

For families with employed partners, the wage freeze of the early 1980s had a significant negative impact on their incomes, while the restructuring of the late 1980s meant that families with parents or partners out of employment had the lowest incomes. These families are also, by chance, those with higher average numbers of dependent children. Childless families were, by contrast more favoured. Finally, there are differences by ethnicity, with Maori families being relatively disadvantaged by comparison with Pakeha. Maori sole parents aged 15-29 years were consistently at the bottom.

Vulnerability, therefore, is a result of a combination of the family's capacity to gain employment and their family size. The passing of responsibility for the welfare burden from the state to the so-called core family will have exacerbated these trends. Moreover, such policies fail to recognise the fact that, for a mix of economic and demographic reasons, some families may be vulnerable across a number of dimensions of their lives. For example, a Pacific Island father aged about 40 years has a high probability not only of being unemployed himself, but of having to support an unemployed teenager (Jackson, 1994).

Towards a Conclusion

The family is undergoing radical change. My generation may not always feel easy about some of these, although we must accept that others, notably changes in patterns of reproduction, represent a reprise of very conservative behaviours. Thus we must be very careful when diagnosing and prescribing, for, when viewed alongside what our parents did and what our children are doing, our own patterns of early childbearing accompanied by rushing into marriage, constituted a deviant trend.

Beyond this, the variable we are analysing, the family, is itself difficult to define and its trends difficult to measure. In part this is because we have drawn on European statistical concepts, which do not reflect different family forms even in Europe itself (cf Murphy, in press). Moreover, we must recognise that, as I have shown, in a multi-cultural society not only is one dealing with culturally determined differentials, but also each ethnic group follows different demographic strategies of family formation.

The family changes I have described may, in part, be viewed as bad news. Firstly, what is overwhelming bad news is the decline in the economic capacity of families to meet changes in their situation. Secondly, assuming that sole parenting is likely to lead to disadvantage, the recent increases in this category may also be seen as undesirable, although I have shown here that the reality does not always fit the stereotype.

In contrast, some of the news is good, notably the decline in teenage pregnancy which seems linked to higher levels of marital dissolution later in life. Moreover, I have shown that some of the perceptions about the family, notably concern about the demise of parenting are misplaced. At least in part the decrease in the number of parenting families, especially at age 30-44 years, is an artefact of demographic squeezes produced by the switch to delayed childbearing.

APPENDIX ONE

Comments on The Newsletter of The Aotearoa / New Zealand International Year of The Family (March/April 1994)

A.   'Sole parents are now 26% of all families'

[COMMENT: The Newsletter confuses 'households' with 'families'. The number of families exceeds the number of households, because of sole parent families which are part of 'extended family/parents plus others' households. Forty-seven percent of Pacific Island, and 39 percent of Maori sole parent families lived in extended family households in 1991. The Newsletter authors exaggerated sole parenting by taking as their numerator all sole parent families, including those in extended family households, but used all households as the denominator]

B.   'One Parent families now make up 26% of the population'

[COMMENT: This is clearly nonsense as it is just the figure in A (above) re-stated with even more inaccuracy. What is of particular concern, however, is the fact that this wildly wrong statistic was picked up and widely circulated over the media, notably commercial stations, and produced a great deal of comment about the DPB. The real figure, including persons in sole parent families within extended households is SEVEN percent]

C.   'Our birthrate is increasing only slowly at 0.9%'

[COMMENT: The authors copied the wrong figure from the 1993 YEARBOOK (p.69)!! The figure quoted refers to natural increase (the sum of the births minus the deaths). In fact the birth rate is DECREASING slowly, from 17.9 per 1000 (1990) to 17.6 (1991)]

D.   '68% of women work full time compared with nearly 92% of men'

[COMMENT: in 1991, 68% of women who are employed worked full time]

The Population Studies Centre wrote to the Committee on April 26 1994 noting these errors, and offering to write a correction. The offer was not picked up.

APPENDIX TWO

Excerpt From Engagements Column, *New Zealand Herald,*
one Saturday in October 1995

'Jocelyn and Shane announce
with glee,
We're engaged and about to
become three'

ACKNOWLEDGEMENTS

In preparing this paper Kim Johnstone prepared the tabulations for me on children in household types. I also benefited from the work of Natalie Jackson, whose work authored by her alone or with me provide much of the data for this paper.

REFERENCES

Alan Guttmacher Inst. 1990. *Induced Abortion: A World Review.* New York.

Boyd, M. and Pryor, E. 'The Cluttered Nest: The Living Arrangements of Young Canadian Adults', *Canadian Journal of Sociology.* 14,4. 461-77

Cliquet, R. 1990. 'The Second Demographic Transition: Fact or Fiction?' *Population Studies*, NO 23. Strasbourg, Council of Europe

Coleman, D. 1992. 'European Demographic Systems of the Future: Convergence or Diversity?', *Human Resources in Europe At the Dawn of the Twenty-First Century.* Luxembourg, Office of Official Publications of the European Communities. 137-79.

Demographic Trends 1993. Statistics New Zealand.

Hoem, J. M. 1990. 'Social Policy and the Recent Fertility Change in Sweden', *Population and Development Review*, 16,4, 735-48.

Interdepartmental Committee on Population Policy Guidelines 1990. *The Human Face of New Zealand.* Wellington, Statistics New Zealand.

Jackson, N. 1994. 'Youth Unemployment and the 'Invisible Hand': A Case for a Social Measure of Unemployment', in P.S. Morrison (ed) *Labour, Employment and Work in New Zealand.* Proceedings of the Sixth Conf. 24-25 Nov. Wellington, Vic. Univ. 177-88.

Jackson, N. and Pool, I. 1994. *Fertility and Family Formation in the Second Demographic Transition: New Zealand Patterns and Trends*. Wellington, NZ Inst for Soc. Res. and Dev.

Jackson, N. and Pool, I. In press. 'Will the Real New Zealand Family Please Stand Up? Substantive and Methodological Factors affecting Research and Policy on Families and Households', *NZ Journal of Social Policy*.

Jackson, N., Pool, I. & Cheung, M.C.C. 1994. 'Maori and Non-Maori Fertility: Convergence, Divergence, or Parallel Trends?', *New Zealand Population Review*, 20,1&2, 31-57.

Johnstone, K. and Pool, I. Under editorial review. 'New Zealand Families: Size, Income Labour Force Participation', contribution to Koopman-Boyden, P., Pool, I., St John, S. & Shirley, I. Paper for Volume One of OUP Series on Families and Social Policy. Oxford, Clarendon.

Lesthaeghe, R. 1991. 'The Second Demographic Transition in Western Countries: An Interpretation', InterUniversity Program in Demography, Working Papers. 1991-2. Brussels.

Lesthaeghe, R. and Moors, G. 1995. 'Is there a New Conservatism that will bring back the Old Family? Ideational Trends and the Stages of Family Formation in Germany, France, Belgium and the Netherlands, 1981-90', InterUniversity Program in Demography, Working Papers 1995-1. Brussels

Martin, B. 1995. 'The New Zealand Family and Restructuring in the 1980s', *Discussion Papers*, No.4. Hamilton, Population Studies Centre, Univ of Waikato.

Mathews, G. 1984. *Le Choc Demographique*. Montreal, Boreal.

Murphy, M. 1993. 'The Contraceptive Pill and Female Employment as Factors in Fertility Change in Britain, 1963-80: A Challenge to the Conventional View', *Population Studies*. 47,2. 221-44

Murphy, M. In Press. 'Household and Family Structures among Ethnic Minority Groups in Britain', in Coleman, D. and Salt, J. (eds) *Ethnic Minorities in Britain: Census* Vol 1,. London.

Pool, I. 1991. *Te Iwi Maori: A New Zealand Population, Past Present and Projected*. Auckland, Univ. Press

Pool, I. 1992. 'The New Zealand Family: Structural Changes in the Context of Shifts in Societal Values', *NZ Population Review*. 18, 1-2. May/Nov, 69-86.

Pool, I. and Crawford 1980. 'Adolescent Ex-Nuptial Births and Ex-Nuptial Conceptions in New Zealand', *NZ Population Review*. 6,2. 20-28.

Pool, I., Davies, L. and Jackson, N. 1993. 'Demographic Change and Family Policy: A Methodological Comment', Paper, Conference on Comparative Research on Welfare States in Transition, Oxford Univ. 9-12 Sept.

Pool, I. and Moore, M. 1986. *Lone Parenthood: Characteristics and Determinants*. Ottawa, Statistics Canada

Roussel, L. 1994. 'Fertility and the Family', in ECE (eds) *European Population Conference, Proceedings*. Vol I. New York and Geneva, United Nations. 35-110

Santow, G. 1989. 'A Sequence of Events in Fertility and Family Formation?' *In-*

ternational Union for the Scientific Study of Population, Conference New Delhi. Liege, IUSSP. vol III 217-29.

Santow, G. and Bracher, M. 1994 . 'First Marital Unions in Australia', *Population Studies*. 48, 1.Nov. 475-96

Sceats, J. and Parr, A. 1995. 'Induced Abortion: National Trends and a Regional Perspective', Paper presented Abortion Providers Conference, Wellington. June.

Sceats, J. and Pool, I. 1985. 'Fertility Regulation', in ESCAP Population Div.(eds) *Population of New Zealand*. New York, United Nations.

van de Kaa, D. 1988. *The Second Demographic Transition Revisited: Theories and Expectations*. Werkstukken, Wassenar, Netherlands Inst. for Advanced Study in the Social Sciences.

Research on the Effect of Marital Transitions on Children

Professor Anne B. Smith
Director, Children's Issues Centre
University of Otago

We chose the area of marital transitions to start our seminar series because it touches so many families in New Zealand from every walk of life, and affects the work of many professionals working with families or children. Yet it is an area where there is a limited amount of New Zealand based research but which affects many policy decisions.

What I would like to do today is to look at some of the research findings about the effect of marital changes on children's development and well being. First I would like to explain why I talk about 'marital transitions' and what I mean by the term. Marital transitions are defined as changes in family structure or composition as a result of the breakdown of a relationship. Marital transitions also include re-partnering but because of the limited time I have this morning I am going to concentrate on breakdowns. It is important first to see divorce and separation within the wider context of society (an **ecological** approach) and not to label divorced families as deviant but to look at processes within families (a **family systems** approach).

An ecological approach on development emphasises that different contexts, and relationships between contexts, have a major influence on development. There are many environmental influences on children – first of all their immediate experiences in home, neighbourhood and school; secondly indirect influences like parental employment, parents' friendship and family support networks; thirdly relationship between custodial and non-custodial home environments and with schools; and finally society's system of policy and values – laws, customs, policies and cultural values about divorce or separation are part of this.

Why is the notion of transition so important in ecological theory? Because, according to Bronfrenbrenner, transitions result in changes in roles, activities and interpersonal relationships, all of which have a profound effect on children's development. He defined ecological transitions as **'whenever a person's position in the ecological environment is altered as a result of a change in role, setting or both'** (1979, p.26). Role changes involve changes in expectations associated with different positions in society, and have 'magiclike power to alter how a person is treated, how she acts, what she does, and thereby even what she thinks and feels' (1979, p.6).

The ecological transitions which occur when a relationship between parents breaks down are major ones in the life of most families. When parents separate more than just one transition occur. From the perspective of the child consider the possible changes:

1. Perhaps the most important transition (for most children in at least the short term) is the move to having one parent responsible for their day-to-day caregiving. That parent may very well be suffering major emotional and psychological trauma, and has to deal with many issues in relation to separation all of which are likely to affect parenting style and interactions with children. When a divorce occurs it means not only the loss of patterns of everyday family interaction and a family member but loss of a way of life. There is an increase in uncertainty and major alterations in the expectations, life experiences and sense of self in both parents and children. Household routines break down, parents experience task overload, children have to take on additional responsibilities, mothers must begin working or increase their workload. The changes do not have to be negative as there may be a transition from being with two parents who have an unhappy, conflictual or even violent relationship to a calmer and happier situation.

2. There is also usually a continuing relationship with the non-custodial parent to adjust to – this relationship will be maintained in different places, times and in different roles (especially with a non custodial parent). This is one of the crucial ingredients in the adjustment to marital transition.

3. The marital break usually involves a change in material circumstances – if the family property is divided, the family home may have to be sold. The evidence seems to be that there is a significant drop in income for most custodial parents (if they are women) after a marital break-up (Maxwell, 1990). If this happens there are some major changes to children's lives – they may have to move houses, schools, neighbourhoods, their mother may have to change her work status (e.g. from being at home to getting a paid job). Each of those changes will mean a different network of relationships with people (teacher, friends, neighbours, workmates) as well as different physical environments. If there is a drop in family income then some of the opportunities for activities previously open to children may be closed. For example the family may not be able to afford music lessons, sporting activities, educational toys and games, home computers, books and other commodities.

4. It is not uncommon for parental separation to be associated with new relationships for one or both parents. So if dad moves away from home he may well have a new partner and the child must develop a relationship with the new partner, and possibly with the partner's children and family.

Divorce should not be viewed as a discrete event but as part of a series of family transitions and changes in family relationships. The response to any family transition will depend both on what precedes and follows it. Researchers are recognising that viewing marital disruption as a sudden event ignores a complex series of family processes that influence the shape of children's lives. Divorce may only crystallise or highlight long standing problems – it may not be a crash but a gradual disentegration. The response to divorce and life in a single-parent household will be influenced by individual adjustment and the quality of family relationships **before** the divorce as well as circumstances surrounding and following the divorce. Divorce in some families may trigger a series of adverse transactional factors such as economic decline, parenting stress and physical and psychological dysfunction. For others it may present an escape from conflict and an unsatisfying marital relationship and a chance for personal growth. There is evidence that differences before divorce have an important effect on children's development (Furstenberg & Teitler, 1994). Much of the research has over-estimated the effect of divorce on children because it ignores conditions prior to divorce.

A Family Systems Approach – From Family Damage to Family Challenge

An ecological approach fits very well with a family systems approach. Froma Walsh (1993) argues for a re-examination of the assumptions about 'normal families'. The family systems approach suggests that there are multiple influences on family functioning and argues against a deficit model of the family. What we mean by the term 'normal' and how we feel families 'ought to be' is measured by the our cultural and societal frame of reference. Even the definition of family is questionable because the nature of the family changes constantly. Some people still see the 'normal' family as the one on the cornflakes packet ('self-contained within the boundaries of the white picket fence') with dad providing the financial support, mum the caring and domestic support and two children (preferably a boy and a girl). Every generation worries about the stability and continuity of the family and thinks it is seeing the breakdown of the family. Indeed the ideal family was not at all ideal, especially for women, since their responsibility for maintaining the family came at great personal cost.

> Nostalgia for a lost family tradition that never existed has distorted our perceptions and fuelled the myth that any deviation from the idealised normal family is inherently pathological (Walsh, p.15).

This nostalgia has driven research to look for the harmful effects of divorce on children's development and sees families not fitting the stereotype of normality as deviant. Allen (1993) criticises research on the effect of marital disruption on children's well being. She says that the findings reveal how complicated, variable, and diverse within-family experiences are and that the labelling of children of divorce is also harmful and unhelpful.

> The focus on marital disruption confounds one type of life course transition with other factors that may be far more detrimental to children's well-being, such as father abandonment, neglect, and failure to pay child support...The real culprits in children's

lives are persistent poverty, conflict, neglect, abuse, and abandonment, not parental divorce. A more salient question than the negativity of marital disruption is: What societal supports, household arrangements, and family relationships and processes assist children in dealing with inevitable life transitions? (Allen, 1993, p.2)

The tendency has been to blame families (especially mothers) for the problems of delinquency, lack of school achievement, unemployment, poverty, and violence whereas these problems within the family are a **result** rather than a cause of societal upheaval. It is a problem that most studies of divorce do not allow a determination of causality and are based on correlational data.

Research on the Effects of Marital Disruption

Amato & Keith (1991a) reviewed 92 studies comparing samples of children living in single parent families with children living in intact families on measures of well being. (see Table 1). 70 percent of these studies showed negative effects of divorce on children's well being but the effects were not large. The biggest negative effects were on father-child relations and conduct. Studies which were more methodologically sound (e.g. had control groups, large samples and

---

Table 1: Parental Divorce and the Well-being of Children: A Meta-Analysis.

Amato, P.R. & Keith, B. (1991) *Psychological Bulletin, 110* (1), pp. 26-46

Comparisons of Children From Divorced and Intact Families Across Various Domains of Well-Being: Mean Effect Sizes, Fail-Safe N Values, and Homogeneity Values

Domain of Well-being	N	Mean Effect Size	Fail-safe N	H_T
School achievement	39	−.16*	855	85.6*
Conduct	56	−.23*	3,474	221.5*
Psychological adjustment	50	−.08*	464	98.6*
Self-concept	34	−.09*	111	87.2*
Social adjustment	39	−.12*	506	219.4*
Mother-child relations	22	−.19*	212	86.8*
Father-child relations	18	−.26*	456	73.0*
Other	26	.06		51.1*

Note: N refers to the number of effect sizes based on independent samples. A negative effect size indicates that the divorced group scores lower than the intact group in well-being. H_T is the Hedges and Olkin (1985) measure of homogeneity.

* $p < .001$

controlled for social class and other variables such as income) showed weaker effects of divorce than poorer quality studies. The effects were not different according to gender, but there were age differences suggesting more negative effects for children in primary and secondary school (compared to preschool and university). More recent studies showed weaker effects than older studies (going back to the fifties) suggesting that the consequences of divorce become less serious with time. Divorce has become more common and more accepted during the last 30 years and this may have led to fewer negative effects on children.

Table 2: The Consequences of Parental Divorce and Adult Well-being: A Meta-Analysis.

Amato, P.R. & Keith, B. (1991)
Journal of Marriage and the Family, 53, pp. 43-58

Data on Mean Effect Sizes for Comparisons of Adult Subjects
from Divorced and Intact Family Backgrounds Across
15 Domains of Well-being

Domain of Well-being	n	X Effect Size	Fail-safe N	H
Psychological adjustment	23	−.32***	1,594	388.51***
Behaviour/conduct	9	−.28***	418	37.36***
Self-concept	3	−.09		2.74
Use of mental health services	6	−.21***	26	5.41
Social relations	8	−.06**	25	15.67*
Parent-child relations	13	−.02		21.71*
Marital quality	16	−.13***	141	12.92
Separation or divorce	24	−.22***	1,995	113.99***
General family quality	5	−.12***	29	12.36*
One-parent family status	6	−.36***	313	84.91***
Educational attainment	18	−.28***	1,263	38.03**
Material quality of life	10	−.18***	112	22.74**
Occupational quality	9	−.11***	36	21.88**
Physical health	11	−.10***	76	13.74
Other	6	−.10***	48	36.35***

Note: n refers to the number of effect sizes based on independent samples. A negative effect size indicates that the divorced group scores lower than the intact group in well-being. *H* is the Hedges and Olkin (1985) measure of heterogeneity.

* $p < .05$.   ** $p < .01$.   *** $p < .001$.

Children from divorced families did less well than children who had lost a parent through death; but children with step-parents did not do better than children with single parents (in fact there was a slight tendency in the other direction).There was an interesting finding, though that boys in step-parent families did better than boys in divorced families; while girls in step-parent families did not do so well as girls in divorced families. These results do suggest that the addition of a stepfather may be positive but for boys only. The study concluded that:

> ...parental divorce may be a stressor that, in the larger scheme of things, has relatively minor effects on most children (Amato & Keith, 1991a, p.40).

Amato & Keith (1991b) also carried out a meta-analysis of 37 studies which looked at the outcomes of divorce in adulthood. (See Table 2.) Again the effects were negative but not large. Out of 169 separate comparisons of outcomes 89 percent of the effect sizes were negative – 45 percent were significant and negative and only 1 percent were significant and positive. There was evidence that the more recent the study the less strong the negative effect, that the negative effects were stronger for whites than for blacks but there were no differences according to gender. The authors say that the outcomes show divorce is associated with poorer psychological well-being (depression and low life satisfaction), family well-being (lower marital quality), socioeconomic well-being (educational attainment, income and occupational prestige), and physical health. The racial differences may be due to the general prevalence of single parenthood for black families – also the lowering of quality of life may only be a marginal additional negative influence for black compared to white families, because of the greater number of other disadvantaging factors. They argue that **the literature does show that divorce is associated with problems in adult life but that the effect size is weak – i.e. there are not huge differences between divorced and intact families.**

Why does Divorce Impact on Children?

Another more recent study by Amato (1993) attempts to look in more depth at five different theoretical perspectives on children's adjustment to divorce. (See Table 3.) Amato analysed 180 studies dealing with the effect of divorce on children from five possible theoretical perspectives (suggesting different hypotheses). He looks at whether studies support or do not support different hypotheses arising out of different theoretical perspective. (Support means that there is at least one significant finding in favour of the hypothesis.)

1. The Parent Loss Perspective

This theory says that a family with two parents is a better environment for children because it provides better resources for the child (emotional support, practical guidance, information, supervision; a strong authority structure; two role models from which they can learn social skills such as compromise, negotiation and co-operation). Children usually experience a decrease in the quantity and

	Table 3: Divorce and Children's Well-being (Amato, 1993)	
	Studies *Support*	*Studies* *Not Support*
Parental loss		
▶ frequent contact helps	16	16
▶ substitute adult helps	3	0
▶ remarriage helps	11	19
▶ older children OK	8	18
▶ death worse	15	9
Parental adjustment		
▶ custodial parent adjusts well	13	2
▶ good childrearing skills	19	1
▶ quality of relationship with parent	2	1
▶ improves over time920		
Interparental conflict		
▶ high intact same	18	3
▶ lower pre-divorce as well	3	0
▶ worse if continues post-divorce	25	3
▶ improves over time	9	20
Economic hardship		
▶ income helps adjustments	6	5
▶ low intact same	5	2
▶ better if Father has custody	5	10
▶ improves if Mother remarries	11	19
Life stresses		
▶ number of stressful events during and after	10	3
▶ lower if parents remarry	14	16
▶ lower if multiple divorces	2	1

quality of contact with their non-custodial parent after divorce and the decline in parental support is thought to increase problems of poor academic achievement, low self-esteem, misbehaviour.

Predictions and Results

(a) Custodial Parent Contact: 16 studies support the hypothesis that contact with the non-custodial parent is positively associated with positive outcomes. But 16 studies did not support the hypothesis. Some studies show increased problems for children. The impact of non-custodial parent contact may depend on the level of conflict or hostility between spouses.

(b) Other Adult Contact: Contact with another adult (either stepparent or someone else living with mother) can substitute for contact from the absent parent – 3 studies do support this and none do not. The number of adults with whom the child engages in task oriented activities is positively related to adjustment.

(c) Step-parents: If the custodial parent remarries then children should be coping better. Eleven studies support this and 19 studies find kids with step-parents are more poorly adjusted. Six of the studies showed that the presence of a stepfather improves the well being of boys but has no effect on girls.

(d) Timing: The hypothesis is that children experience more problems when parental loss occurs early (when kids are younger) rather than late. Eight studies support it but 18 do not. There is little support for the hypothesis since most studies show no difference. Some studies show that divorce when children are older is more problematic. Young children exhibit more disruptive acting out behaviour whereas older children show more signs of depression.

(e) Death versus Divorce: The fifth hypothesis is that children who lose a parent through death have lower well being than children who lose a parent through divorce. Both parental divorce and death are related to lower child well being although some studies show that divorce but not death has negative outcomes. The weight of the evidence (15 studies versus 9) shows that well being is lowest in divorced families, intermediate in bereaved families and highest in intact families.

Overall **there is modest support for the parental loss perspective** – parental loss may be factor but it cannot on its own account for the well being of children of divorce.

2. Parental Adjustment Hypothesis

This theory suggests that the important factor is the psychological adjustment of the custodial parent. Parents who are supportive and exercise a moderate degree of control facilitate children's development. The stress of divorce is thought, from this perspective, to impair the quality of childrearing skills and to have negative consequences.

(a) Adjustment of Custodial Parent: The hypothesis is that children's well being is related to the psychological adjustment of the custodial parent. 3 studies support this hypothesis, 2 do not.

(b) Quality of Parent/Child Relationship: The hypothesis is that the quality of relationship with the custodial parent affects child adjustment. An overwhelming majority of the studies (19 versus 1) support this hypothesis.

(c) Statistical Controls for Adjustment: Differences in well being are reduced by statistical controls for parental psychological adjustment, quality of childrearing skills and quality of parent-child relationship. (2 in support 1 does not). There are substantially less pronounced differences in the child well being of children from divorced and non-divorced families when these factors are controlled (in 2 studies).

(d) Time since Divorce: Because parents gradually adjust to divorce it can be expected that their childrearing skills will improve with the passage of time since marital dissolution, and hence that the well being of children will increase in time. Nine studies support this hypothesis and 20 do not. Most studies find no association between length of time since divorce and children's well being. Some find a negative relationship. There is little support for this hypothesis.

Overall the parental adjustment hypothesis receives some support though there is some confounding by data being provided by mothers on their own and child adjustment (i.e. the data sources are not independent).

3. Interparental Conflict Perspective

Numerous studies show that an unhappy home environment with high levels of marital discord is not good for children. Children react to interparental hostility with negative emotions such as fear, anger and distress. They feel drawn in and that they have to take sides; there is inappropriate modelling of physical and verbal aggression and many children blame themselves. This perspective holds that conflict between parents prior to and during dissolution is responsible for child's lowered well being and that children in conflict ridden families will be better off after divorce, provided they are then shielded from further conflict.

(a) Conflict in all Families: The first hypothesis is that high conflict intact families have more child problems than low conflict intact families. 18 studies supported this and 3 did not. Many studies show that conflict, not divorce, is associated with poor outcomes. This suggests a very general effect of conflict regardless of family structure.

(b) Pre-divorce Conflict: The second hypothesis is that because marital conflict precedes divorce, children have a lower level of well being. All three studies supported this – and none did not support it. Cherlin using national longitudinal data sets found that children in divorced families had more behaviour problems and lower academic test scores than did children in intact families. However these differences were apparent prior to divorce, and controlling for pre-divorce differences removed most of the effects.

(c) Post-divorce Conflict: Because conflict may continue after divorce children's well being is inversely correlated to the level of post-divorce conflict. 25 studies support this and only 3 do not. Co-operation and low conflict between parents predicts positive divorce adjustment.

(d) Time since Divorce: The fourth hypothesis is that children's adjustment is correlated with the length of time since divorce – most longitudinal studies support this but most cross sectional studies do not. This may be for a number of reasons – first if children drop behind in school they may find it hard to catch up, second divorce may set in motion events that are problematic for children's well being; and third divorce may not end conflict.

Overall there is strong evidence in support for the Conflict hypothesis. Probably the most important variable in predicting how children cope with divorce is the continuing relationship between ex-spouses.

4. The Economic Hardship Perspective

This perspective assumes that the economic hardship brought about by marital dissolution is primarily responsible for the problems faced by children of divorce. Most mothers are worse off economically after divorce and since most children are with their mothers this may adversely affect children's nutrition, health and education. **Most studies show that part of the association between divorce and children's well being can be attributed to education and occupational status – but not all** but there are still significant associations between divorce and children's well being.

(a) Family income is positively related to adjustment in single parent families. Six studies show that income is positively related to academic achievement, good behaviour, psychological adjustment, self concept and social relations but 4 say that there is no difference. One study finds income negatively related to child adjustment.

(b) Statistical Controls for Income: The differences between children from divorced and intact families disappear when income is held constant. 5 studies support this and two do not.

(c) Father Custody: Because fathers are better off than mothers, children of divorced families should be better off with their fathers, according to this hypothesis. Five studies support this and ten do not. Most studies show no difference in well being between children in mother and father custody. A few studies show boys better off in father custody – the results suggest the importance of having a same sex parent rather than economic explanation.(Otherwise daughters should also benefit from father custody).

(d) Remarriage: It is predicted that children from divorced families do better if mothers remarry. 1 study supports this and 19 do not. Some find that remarriage improves the outcome for boys – hence this does not really support an economic perspective.

Overall **relevant studies are too few to provide strong support for the economic hardship perspective – however economic hardship definitely does make a difference**.

5. The Life Stress Perspective

This is the most general perspective which argues that divorce has negative effects for children because of all the life stresses it involves. All of the factors noted above, the loss of a parent, the deteriorating quality of relationships, exposure to conflict and decline in living standards are all Stressors. Furthermore divorce is associated with other events, like changing schools, homes, giving up pets and loss of contact with grandparents – all of these may be distressing. The accumulation of negative events may cause problems for children.

(a) Number of Stressful Events: The first hypothesis is that the well-being of children of divorce is related to the number of stressful events they are exposed to. Ten studies support this – 3 do not suggesting that it may not be the absolute number of changes but the type of change that is important.

(b) Remarriage: The well being of children is lower for children whose parents remarry. Studies are equally split between support and non support for this (14 vs 16). Step-parent problems are more likely when the child is the same sex as the stepparent but present few problems or even benefits for opposite sex children.

(c) Multiple Divorces: The well being of children of divorce is lower for those who experience multiple divorces compared to a single one. Two studies support this hypothesis and one does not.

In summary **support for the stressful life events perspective is strong**.

The strongest and most consistent support is given to the Parental Conflict model. Divorce may actually improve well-being if it decreases hostility between parents.

Children who experience minimal loss of resources and minor stress following divorce are unlikely to experience a decrease in well-being. Indeed, they may even benefit if stress decreases or resources increase following divorce (Amato, 1993, p.36).

Factors which Ameliorate the Negative Effects of Divorce on Children

Support for Parents

Bronfrenbrenner (1979) argued that one of the most important things in supporting positive parenting is the presence of other third parties for backing up the person who takes the main responsibility for parenting. He used the metaphor of a 3 legged stool – where the existence of third party support keeps the stool upright. One result of divorce can be diminished capacity to be an effective parent (Hetherington & Camara, 1984). Parents often feel angry, preoccupied, anxious, distressed or depressed and this makes it difficult to focus on the child's needs and be a warm and supportive parent. It is therefore very important for the parent to have support in maintaining self-sufficiency and competence as a parent. Support for parents from ex-spouse, friends, grandparents, other family members, housekeepers, childcare centres is very important. The capacity of the mother to have positive relationships and support her children, is strongly influenced by other people. Social support facilitates the parenting role and is associated with greater life satisfaction, personal growth and less distress for parents (Hetherington & Camara, 1984).

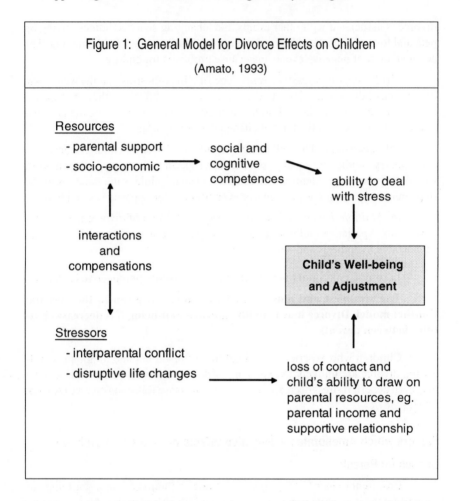

Figure 1: General Model for Divorce Effects on Children
(Amato, 1993)

The combination of low income and lack of social support has been shown to have a particularly negative influence on parenting and to provide a high risk situation for children. Hashima & Amato (1994) found that parents punitive behaviour (yelling, slapping or spanking children) was related to poverty and isolation. When people on low incomes felt that they could rely on people for informal assistance this seemed to buffer them from inappropriate parenting. Lack of both social and economic support may intensify feelings of hopelessness and vulnerability for parents which then influences the way that they interact with their children.

Support for Children

It is interesting that Bronfrenbrenner put such a strong emphasis on support for the parent but very little on such support for children. Warm, loving support and care from parents is probably the most crucial support for the child in adjusting to divorce. Brown et al (1993) looked at family functioning in relation to children's adjustment to divorce. They found that the best predictors (accounting for almost half of the variance) of children's adjustment to divorce were measures of positive family relationships included maintaining family rituals, providing a sense of security for the child, supporting each other emotionally and maintaining the organisation of the family. The study shows the importance of providing resources, nurturance and support for children in families where there has been a separation. Children adjust better to divorce when the relationship between ex-spouses and between parent and child remain open, empathetic and relatively free of conflict, when children can appreciate the continuity of their relationship with both parents, and avoid taking responsibility for the breakup.

Schools and early childhood centres can also offer support to children undergoing stressful experiences. Hetherington et al (1982) found that in the 2 years after divorce children's social and cognitive development was enhanced if children were in schools with explicitly defined schedules, rules and regulations, with consistent warm discipline and clear expectations for behaviour. Under stress children seem to benefit from a structured, safe and predictable environment. Staff can validate the self-worth, competence, and personal control of children.

The presence of social support in the child's social environment has also been shown to help children cope with separation and divorce (Bouchard & Drapeau, 1991; Wyman et al, 1985). Bouchard & Drapeau found that children from divorced families had less dense support networks than children from intact families. They had a tendency to feel less secure and integrated into their social environment. Adult friends, mother's new partners, babysitters and teachers can play an important role in supporting children from separated families. Where children have wider and denser social support networks (ie more connections between their family and friends) and significant relationships with others are preserved, children adjust better. The authors suggest that:

> ...maintaining as many intact links as possible between children's family members and their social networks as well as encouraging close relationships among the children's friends... Keeping in touch with previous neighbors and family-in-law members, moving, if necessary, but to a close location, attending the same school, perpetuating the same holiday habits and installing a living routine may have a huge impact on children's psychological adjustment. This... may enhance a feeling of stability and coherence in their lives (Bouchard & Drapeau, 1991, p.273).

Teja & Stolberg (1993) found a consistent relationship between 9 to 12 year-old children's peer support and their adjustment to divorce. Their friends' support was a major protector of children from the stress of divorce and this became increasingly important as children got older. The centrality of family relationships decline compared to peer relationships at around 12 years of age. The study reinforces the importance of maintaining a steady and stable peer friendship network for children after divorce or separation to help children differentiate themselves from parents and become independent.

Custody, Contact and Co-Parental Relations

The relationships between family members does not usually end when a divorce occurs. Relationships are usually altered rather than completely terminated. For example, husband and wife usually continue to interact in some way in relation to supporting continuing contact with children and decisions about children. Also, most non-custodial parents wish to continue a relationship with their children. Non-custodial fathers often become increasingly less available to their children but non custodial mothers are more likely to retain contact with their children.

A survey by the Department of Justice of 490 couples (Lee, 1991) showed that in 80 per cent of cases following divorce the custodial parent was the mother. By two years after separation, however, 25 percent of children (according to custodial respondents) were not seeing their non-custodial parent at all. About 40 percent of non-custodial parents saw their children about once a fortnight. Most parents (more non custodial than custodial) felt that children enjoyed and were not upset by these visits. There have been similar findings of relatively low contact in American studies (Wallerstein & Kelly, 1980; Hetherington et al, 1993; Furstenberg & Nord, 1985) and many authors conclude that marital disruption can effectively destroy ongoing relationships between children and non-custodial parents. Australian research (Brown, 1994) indicates somewhat higher levels of continuing access in Australia with about two thirds of children still seeing their absent parent regularly.

Previous research suggests that the success of continuing contact between children and non-custodial parents depends very much on the relationship between parents:

> If the noncustodial parent is reasonably well-adjusted, competent in parenting and has a close relationship with the child, and if the child is not exposed to conflict between the two parents, continued contact can have a salutary effect on the child's adjustment. However, it takes an exceptionally close relationship with a noncustodial parent to buffer a child from the deleterious effects of a conflictual, non-supportive relationship with a custodial parent. If there is high conflict between the parents, joint custody and continuing contact can have adverse effects on the child (Hetherington et al, 1993, p.213).

In most cases following divorce it is difficult to achieve successful consensual co-parenting. Hetherington say that the best that can usually be achieved is independent but non interfering parental relations. In a substantial group of families, conflict is sustained or accelerated following divorce and is often associated with diminished contact and fewer child support payments. Children can be 'caught in the middle' – asked to carry messages between parents, inform each parent of the others' activities, to defend one parent against the other's disparaging remarks. As long as children are not involved in parental conflict children are able to cope well even if households have different rules and expectations. Children are able to learn the differing role demands and constraints required to relate to two different home situations. Problems arise when parents try to interfere with each others' child rearing, when children don't want to leave their friends, neighbourhoods or other routines

Summary and Conclusions

To conclude and sum up, there is evidence that divorce and separation are stressful for children and that their well being and development can be adversely affected, although the differences between children in divorced and intact families are quite small, and these effects seem to be diminishing in current social contexts where divorce is an accepted part of many children's experience. I think this quote from Edgar is a realistic appraisal:

> While it is true that Australian studies, and some of the better United States studies, show that divorce in and of itself does not explain the damage done to children's adjustment and well-being. In my view it is absolutely misleading to turn this into a claim that divorce has no damaging effects on children. Time and again the research shows that divorce, of all major family events, is associated with repeated disruptions and disjunctions in the child's life (Edgar, 1993, p.5).

There is limited value, however, in continuing to do more research to identify the negative effects of family structural change on children's adjustment. In my view this is a dead end. Some research shows that children can survive and flourish after family change when their parents are not isolated and unsupported and can provide a warm, accepting but consistent and firm family environment. It is important to look in more depth at the dynamics of families as they come to terms with marital transitions. The value of networks of family, friends and supportive schools and early childhood centres and of continuing meaningful relationships with non custodial parents has been well demonstrated in the research. In my view what we need to be doing is trying to do identify factors which help children and families adjust. It is a particular problem that so little qualitative research has been done to connect these general relationships which have been identified in the literature with the specifics of peoples' lives. We need to know more about the meanings and understandings of the participants in family change, particularly the children. While the rhetoric of the best interests of the child is present there has been very little attempt to talk to children about their experiences and perceptions. The Children's Issues Centre hopes to be able to make a genuine contribution to research, practice and policy by initiating work in this area.

REFERENCES

Allen, K. R. (1993). The Dispassionate Discourse of Children's Adjustment to Divorce. *Journal of Marriage and the Family, 55*.

Amato, P. R. (1993). Children's Adjustment to Divorce: Theories, Hypotheses, and Empirical Support. *Journal of Marriage and the Family, 55,* 23-38.

Amato, P. R. (1993). Family Structure, Family Process, and Family Ideology. *Journal of Marriage and the Family, 55*, 50-54.

Amato, P.R. & Keith, B. (1991a) Parental divorce and the well being of children: a meta-analysis. *Psychological Bulletin, 110* (1), 26-46.

Amato, P. R., & Keith, B. (1991b). Parental Divorce and Adult Well-being: A Meta-analysis. *Journal of Marriage and the Family, 53*, 43-58.

Arditti, J. A., & Keith, T. Z. (1993). Visitation Frequency, Child Support Payment, and the Father-Child Relationship Postdivorce. *Journal of Marriage and the Family, 55*(August 1993), 699-712.

Bouchard, C. & Drapeau, S. (1991). The Psychological Adjustment of Children from Separated Families: The Role of Selected Social Support Variables. *Journal of Primary Prevention, 11* (4), 259-276.

Bronfrenbrenner, U. (1979) *The Ecology of Human Development.* Cambridge: Harvard University Press.

Brown, J. H., Eichenberger, S.A., Portes, P.R. and Christensen, D.N. (1991). Family Functioning Factors Associated with the Adjustment of Children of Divorce. *Journal of Divorce & Remarriage, 17* (1/2), 81-95.

Brown, C. (1994). The Impact of Divorce on Families. *Family and Conciliation Courts Review, 32* (2), 149-167.

Buchanan, C.M., Maccoby, E.E. & Dornbusch, S.M. (1991) Caught between parents: Adolescents' experiences in divorced homes. *Child Development, 26*, 1008-1029.

Camara, K. A., & Resnick, G. (1989). Styles of Conflict Resolution and Cooperation Between Divorced Parents: Effects on Child Behavior and Adjustment. *American Journal of Orthopsychiatry, 59* (4), 560-575.

Edgar, D. (July 1993). *Joint Parenting Systems: A Critical Assessment from the Child's Point of View.* Paper presented at the 1st World Congress on Family Unit and Children's Rights, Sydney, Australia.

Furstenberg, F. F., & Nord, C. W. (1985). Parenting Apart: Patterns of Childrearing After Marital Disruption. *Journal of Marriage and the Family, 47*, 893-904.

Furstenberg, F. P., & Teitler, J. O. (1994). Reconsidering the Effects of Marital Disruption: What Happens to Children of Divorce In Early Adulthood? *Journal of Family Issues, 15* (2), 173-190.

Hashima, P.Y. & Amato, P.R. (1994) Poverty, social support and parental behaviour. *Child Development, 65* (2), 394-403.

Hetherington, E. M., Cox, M., & Cox, R. (1982). Effects of Divorce on Parents and Children. In M. E. Lamb (Ed.), *Non Traditional Families*, (pp. 233-288). New Jersey: Lawrence Erlbaum.

Hetherington, E. M., & Camara, K. A. (1984). Families in Transition: The Processes of Dissolution and Reconstitution. In R. D. Parke (Ed.), *Review of Child Development Research*, (pp. 399-439). Chicago: University of Chicago Press.

Hetherington, E. M., Law, T. C., & O'Connor, T. G. (1993). Divorce: Challenges, changes and new chances. In F. Walsh (Ed.), *Normal Family Processes*, (pp. 208-234). New York: The Guildford Press.

Johnston, J.R., Kline, M., & Tschann, J.M. (1989) Ongoing postdivorce conflict: Effects on children of joint custody and frequent access. *American Journal of Orthopsychiatry, 59*, 566-592.

Kelly, J. B. (1991). Children's Post-Divorce Adjustment: Effects of conflict, parent adjustment and custody arrangement. *Family Law, February*, 52-56.

Lee, A. (1991). Survey of parents who have obtained a dissolution. *Family Law Bulletin, 2* (Part 12), 149-151.

McDonald, M. (1990) *Children's perceptions of access and their adjustment in the post-separation period.* Family Court of Australia, Office of the Chief Executive, Research Report No 9.

Richards, M. P. M. (1982). Post-divorce Arrangements for Children: A Psychological Perspective. *Journal of Social Welfare Law*, 133-151.

Simons, R. L., Whitbeck, L. B., Beaman, J., & Conger, R. D. (1994). The Impact of Mothers' Parenting, Involvement by Nonresidential Fathers, and Parental Conflict on the Adjustment of Adolescent Children. *Journal of Marriage and the Family, 56* (May 1994), 356-374.

Teja, S. & Stolberg, A.L. (1993). Peer Support, Divorce, and Children's Adjustment. *Journal of Divorce & Remarriage, 20* (3/4), 45-64.

Wallerstein, J. & Kelly, J. (1980) *Surviving the breakup: How children cope with divorce.* New York: Basic Books.

Walsh, F. (1993) Conceptualization of normal family processes. In F. Walsh (Ed.) *Normal Family Processes.* 2nd edition. New York: Guildford Press, 3-69.

Walsh, W. M. (1992). Twenty Major Issues in Remarriage Families. *Journal of Counselling & Development, 70* (July/August 1992), 709-715.

Wolman, R., & Taylor, K. (1991). Psychological Effects of Custody Disputes on Children. *Behavioral Sciences and the Law, 9*, 399-417.

Wyman, P.A., Cowan, L.E., Hightower, A.D. & Pedro-Carroll, J.L. (1985) Perceived competence, self-esteem, anxiety in latency-aged children of divorce. *Journal of Clinical Child Psychology, 58*, 355-378.

The Torn Whariki

Associate Professor Ngapare Hopa
Department of Social Anthropology
University of Waikato

Whanaungatanga

A Torn Whariki is quite a useful metaphor for bringing a Maori perspective to this seminar on 'Supporting Children and Parents Through Family Changes' whether one is discussing tangata whenua in general or, however we may define it, the whanau (family arrangement) in particular.

Applied to the original whariki of the land and to the wear and tear of relationships between tangata whenua and tauiwi, it has been torn in many places, worn threadbare in others and had the edges frayed. Some repair work has occurred of course, old patterns have been adapted, new ones introduced and borders conveniently edged. The process has produced a whariki of diverse materials and motifs reflecting historical and, continuing into the present, the contemporary experience of being Maori in Aotearoa/New Zealand.

It is thus difficult to talk about the 'whanau' aside from the 'whariki' of history and colonisation of Aotearoa. The 'whariki' has been re-shaped, down to its fundamental warp (descent) and wefts (whanaungatanga) – the basis for social organisation, for structuring whanau and the wider kin groupings in which it is embedded.

Among significant determinants has been the astonishing rapidity of change that has occurred in Maori demography. This morning, Professor Pool drew our attention to a number of its key characteristics – e.g. the extent to which change from a high fertility level (by world standards) to a very low fertility rate (by world standards too) has occurred and, all within one generation! Maori have experienced one of the most rapid fertility declines in the 20th century. An ageing population is one critical consequence (Pool, 1991: 170).

According to the 1991 census, the kaumatua population (that proportion of kaumatua aged 65 and over) numbered 10,000 who accounted for less than 3 percent of the total Maori population. By 2021 (little more than a generation away) Maori over 65 are expected to have trebled in number to 31,000. By this time they will account for more than 6 percent of the Maori population (Wereta, 1994: 79-84; Douglas, 1994: 86).

Modernisation

'Modernisation' or 'industrialisation' including such things as changes in attitude, knowledge, ambition, life-style and fertility control, account for some parts of this shift in Maori demographics and convergence toward Pakeha patterns (Pool; 1991: 136-189).

More specifically, are determinants like those spelled out by Douglas (1994: 86):

- greater acceptance and use of contraceptives

- a change in values relating to child-rearing, whereas a generation ago, almost all Maori women had children, and having children was considered not merely normal but universal if not obligatory, in recent years, an increasing proportion of Maori women have chosen not to have children and those who do, have chosen to have fewer

- a greater acceptance of family planning, not merely to plan and space pregnancies but to plan for an ideal family size and composition

- more willingness to seek legal abortions and a realisation of changing attitudes to the value and sanctity of life

- changes in both men and women in their attitudes toward gender roles, resulting in changed attitudes and behaviour both within the household and more widely in community interaction

- shifting attitudes and practises towards marriage, especially inter-ethnic marriages where a spouse comes from a tradition of small nuclear families where kinship is not a central part of social relations, rather than a tradition of large families embedded in an extensive kinship network

He goes on to say that these changes have resulted not only in fewer children per couple, but also in other changes like: the age of the mother at the birth of her first child and of her last leading to a shorter period of the parents' life-time involved in child dependency and consequently to a greater realisation of the cost of parenting (ibid).

Urban migration has also had significant consequences for rural Maori communities. It has been estimated that more than three-quarters of the members of most tribes now live outside their tribal boundaries and, from interpreting the available data, it appears that no major tribe has more than half of its members living at 'home' (Douglas 1994: 91). Among other things, this has had major implications for social organisation, iwi cohesion, kinship, depth of knowledge about tikanga, and identity. One would expect that the whanau would transmit these things to the rangatahi (young), but as the 1991 census revealed, 27 percent of Maori do not know their iwi name or iwi affiliations! What are the implications of state defined 'iwi' settlements for them? If the recent Waikato settlement is any indication, individuals and whanau living within the tribal rohe (region) have to demonstrate their whakapapa connections and become registered on the beneficiary roll held by the Iwi Authority in order to qualify for entitlements.

A Range of Maori Realities

Our situation is compounded: the traditional warp and weft of the social whariki persist to be very meaningful for some Maori and to underpin interpersonal and inter-generational relationships. For other Maori whakapapa (genealogy) and whanaungatanga (relatedness) are being revived or re-discovered, as the basis for identity and claim to iwi affiliation and perhaps entitlements. For still other Maori, these concepts are being given either new meaning or ignored altogether.

That is to say: whakapapa and whanaungatanga appear to mean different things to different people depending on their enculturation, changing life-styles, aspirations and so on. So too with the meaning and function of the whanau.

I say 'appear' because as I tried to point out in a paper back in 1990, we lack quantitative and qualitative research on Maori families critical to addressing the very issues which have inspired this Manawa Rangahau Tamariki Centre and this seminar.

Ignorance of iwi affiliation(s) of whakapapa and whanaungatanga, is only one indication of individuals and whanau who already live in diverse realities and whose homes and household compositions reflect the same. What, for instances of whanau capacities to adapt and cope with caring for, if not one, perhaps several ageing members? How many people are accommodated in one home? Are there occupants parents and children, plus other kin? What are the likely costs if budgets of household members on fixed incomes are already stretched? These among other variables, await research.

Durie's observations on research into Maori health are just as applicable to the whanau (Durie: 1994). He points out that health has been the subject of sectional and cross-sectional research, oriented to specific interests like education, employment or unemployment and based on the assumption that Maori is a definable measure (ibid: 142). In his view, such an assumption may in terms of statistics represent a definable measure, but statistics do not reflect cultural understandings, at least as they apply to the diverse realities of contemporary Maori. Again, these remain to be researched.

What is required is the kind of integrated research which he advocated and demonstrated in his study of Maori Health. To gain a comprehensive picture of Maori health status says Durie, depends on data from several sources. And to talk about Maori health is also to talk about whanau – about interpersonal and inter-generational relationships – and because Maori to not live their lives in narrow sectors, it is difficult to rationalise the whanau apart from the wider Maori and Pakeha context and from demographic, socio-economic and cultural variables therein.

As Durie expressed the matter:

Correlations between socio-economic, cultural, mortality, and morbidity data are needed in order to assess the vitality, the mauri, of Maori individuals and family (ibid).

He goes on to say that 'there is no single Maori reality and a statistical Maori may differ markedly from another Maori in terms of lifestyle, cultural affiliations and health (ibid.). One would concur, but it makes the study of the Maori family that much more complicated. Social reality is rarely tidy, though governments historically and continuing into the present, have attempted to contain the fluidity which has always been a mark of Maori social groupings, by creating neat, convenient and manageable boxes, and then placing Maori into them.

The term Maori itself is a classic example, even though qualifiers have been made more recently. Iwi is another, as the fiscal envelope and one recent settlement confirms (Waikato/Tainui Settlement: 1995).

In the 1990 paper I mentioned earlier, I stressed that the term 'whanau', its adaptation and evolution reflects varying situations, pressures and policy outcomes and thus is a good example of a dynamic and changing social group (Hopa: 1990). There are however, no studies of the dynamics involved, of the sociology of everyday life in Maori households, though the 1992-95 Hoe-nuku-Roa, Maori Profiles Research Project, headed up by Durie is one current study and the School of Social Sciences at Waikato University, multi-disciplinary research proposal on Transactions, Mid-Life Families and Society, is another that promises to fill some gaps.

I will attempt to do the same but will limit my discussion to whanau structures and compositions which some statistics (like the fact that 25 percent of Maori households are composed of two parents plus others) have pointed up and to my own observations which suggest the variations on a 'familial' theme that are emerging in response to the interplay of cultural, demographic and market based processes or compulsions.

The definition of the Maori family provided in the 1994 ICPD Draft Report (p.35) defined the Maori family as 'either a couple with or without a child (or children). That is a pattern which reflects one reality, – a response to the 'urbanisation/modernisation' process.

Another definition describes the whanau as a diffuse unit, usually based on a common sense of descent within which certain responsibilities and obligations are maintained (Durie 1994: 1). The long assumed extended or three generation stem family is illustrative of this familial form, though variations on the theme are emerging.

Thus defined, this extended though fluid family unit, still exists as the primary support system for meeting physical, cultural, financial and emotional needs. The cultural imperatives of respect for age, the view of kaumatua and kuia as repositories of tradition, manaakitanga (care) and the inclusivity of whanaungatanga (relatedness) have been key determinants in the structuring and composition of such households. But so too have the ravages of economic restructuring, been influential. Affordable housing has gone. More and more are whanau unable to cope with house rents and basic overheads. Evictions appear to be increasing, though I have no figures to support this impression.

Where then do people go? To whom do they turn? The elastic walls of Maori homes are becoming even more stretched, such that a 'two parent plus others' household has to expand to accommodate relatives for varying amounts of time – never mind if they eat you out of house and home, run up the toll bill, come for a weekend and end up staying five years!

That is the underside of custom which puts pressure on space and income – every dollar of which has to count. It should be noted that in successive census enumerations, the number of dependants of a Maori wage or salary earner, is much higher than for a non-Maori wage/salary earner. This means that the money earned has to be spread over a greater number of people. And, as if this were not enough, in its wake are pressures that test family interaction, domestic stability and ability to survival.

Today natural grandparent(s) are also choosing to remain independent and not move in with offspring. All the better to pursue individual interests, attend hui free from baby-sitting mokopuna (grand-children) and/or other whanau obligations. Papakainga (housing) development on marae have afforded many this opportunity. Their role in the whanau of their offspring in some cases is being replaced by classificatory grand-aunts or uncles, more distant senior relatives or fictive kin.

Independence may be short lived however, if in a situation of domestic abuse, separation or divorce, the aggrieved goes home with mokopuna entout or leaves mokopuna in the care of grandparents who frequently can ill-afford to keep them, let alone assume other responsibilities for the well-being of mokopuna, especially if they are teenagers given to Country and Western, rapp or Bob Marley! For all their best efforts, grandparents are known to wring their hands in despair and frustration, to resort to abuse themselves and/or to sending their moko back to parents or one or other of them or along the extended family network.

Other variations on the 'household' theme include siblings, brother and sister, widowed or separated and who may have lived in different locations, moving in together to manaaki each other and their dependants financially and emotionally. In such arrangements, the male acts as 'father': to his own and as surrogate authority figure and disciplinarian to his sibling's children.

Another I would describe as a household composed of classificatory adult siblings whose association is grounded in the cultural values of whanaungatanga and manaakitanga, but are also motivated by economic need.

Yet another definition of whanau includes the most rapidly growing type of Maori household headed by a single parent (usually the mother) and her dependent child (ren). According to census figures for 1991, more than one third of all Maori households comprised a single parent and dependent children and more than 30 percent of all Maori children lived in such households. And what is more, the majority of these families relied on income support – either the Domestic Purposes Benefit (DPB) or Unemployment or Sickness and Disability benefits (Douglas: 1994).

For Maori males in the same period, DSW, sickness and disability benefits were a main and increasing source of income. The proportion of Maori male recipients is illustrated by figures covering the decade 1981-1991. The proportion increased from 12 percent to 54 percent of whom half were on unemployment. Twenty eight percent of all Maori males aged 20-39 were on unemployment. (Douglas: 1994).

Add to the problem of Maori males in the 90s is the fact that this narrow age range (20-39) comprise almost half of the Maori labour force and therefore, half of the income earners.

Survival Initiatives

We should not be surprised therefore that tight budgets have led to some creative 'familial arrangements' of people banding together to rent a dwelling and share the costs, thereby diminishing anxiety of stretched and inadequate resources. Such arrangements also allow for collective care and nurturing of children, something that current policy and devolution of responsibility does not encourage.

These associations are an example of yet another definition of whanau, one that allows for a variety of non-traditional situations where Maori with similar interests form a cohesive group woven in the absence of a common line of descent, though in terms of interpersonal relationships, may act as if it did. The term 'bro' and 'cuzzie bro' might be seen to epitomise relationships in this type of household.

The burning question remains – the role of the whanau in child-rearing and support. For a very high proportion of young Maori parents, the state has become their major financial support. And when their energies are directed to simply surviving, under these domestic arrangements, what can we expect in terms of cultural transmission of tikanga or where this has atrophied, coping with the pressures exerted by custom anyway?

The term whanau may thus be seen as encompassing a diversity of 'familial arrangements' responsive to persisting and/or adapted cultural values, demography and the often confusing and contradictory policies of a re-structured economy.

To get a grip on these 'familial forms', we need more and better research into the structure and dynamics of Maori whanau – and not just of Maori households, because whanaungatanga is not confined or defined by co-residency. Equally important is that Maori need to be the prime subject of this research and not just an add-on to research designed for, by and about non-Maori.

Predictions

Can we predict further changes? It has been suggested that a lot can be learned from the culture of poverty and welfare dependence existing in the central city ghettos of Chicago, Los Angeles or New York in the USA and Brixton or Notting Hill Gate in the UK (Douglas, 1994: 92). Julius Wilson's (1987) study of increased joblessness and single parent families in black American urban communities is a case in point. Douglas has summarised Wilson's main arguments and made comparisons with our situation:

1. The structural unemployment hypothesis: states that joblessness has increased among young black males partly because there are fewer unskilled and semi-

skilled blue-collar jobs available. It has been applied to the New Zealand economy and labour market, especially since active re-structuring of the public sector (which was the largest employer of Maori workers) began in earnest in the early 1980s.

2. The non-marriageable men hypothesis: states that the two parent black family is disappearing because male joblessness has made marriage less attractive. This hypothesis has also been applied to New Zealand in relation to the extent to which young Maori men are imprisoned, unemployed or unemployable and are considered a liability rather than an advantage by solo mothers (whose main source of income is the DPB).

3. The physical isolation hypothesis: states that both single parenthood and black joblessness have also increased among poor blacks because the black middle-class has moved out of the ghetto. As a consequence, black inter-city schools have deteriorated, ghetto businesses have closed, the police have fewer allies in their struggle to control crime, job seekers have fewer employed neighbours to help them find jobs and the young have fewer positive role models. The isolation hypothesis has also been applied to New Zealand recently, in relation to the ghettoisation of large tracts of South Auckland and other public housing areas in larger urban areas. It has been applied to employment opportunities and discussed in relation to community support for schools since the abolition of urban zoning.

It goes without saying perhaps, that among other things, urban ghettos are notoriously poverty stricken and their inhabitants powerless. Here in New Zealand, high wage occupations have grown at least 20 percent more rapidly than middle to low wage occupations which not surprisingly, require above average educational qualifications. A new breed of highly paid 'efficiency and cost saving' gurus has emerged, though not necessarily skilled in delivery.

Under the Employment Contracts Act, a vigorous expansion of low wage occupations and part-time work has occurred and, if the level of unemployment is indicative, the economic situation has been particularly bad for the young and inexperienced, especially young Maori (both male and female).

Concluding Remarks

What might the next decade bring? As globalisation proceeds, the social and economic conditions and the status of Maori could improve or deteriorate or remain where it is now. What is certain is that further social engineering will be driven by and be inextricably tied to government policies directed at education, training, employment and income support. Like many minorities marginalised by the hegemony, Maori will survive because of their capacity to adapt and because, despite the barriers yet to be overcome, of their determination to be heard.

Kia ora.

REFERENCES

Douglas, Te Kohu (1977) The New Net Goes Fishing. In J.C. Caldwell (Ed), *The Persistence of High Fertility*. Canberra, Australia, National University.

(1994) Demographic Changes and Their Social Consequences for Maori. In Kia Pumau *Tonu Proceedings of the Hui Whakapumau*, Maori Development Conference, Massey University.

Durie, M. (1994) *Whaiora*. Maori Health Development. Oxford University Press, Auckland.

Hopa, N.K. (1990) From Flax Roots. In G. Maxwell, I. Hassall and J. Robertson, *Toward a Child and Family Policy for New Zealand*. Wright & Carman Ltd, Wellington.

Pool, I. (1991) *Te Iwi Maori*. Auckland University Press, Auckland.

Puketapu, B. (1994) Hokia ki te Kopae a Nga Pahake – The Classical Maori Journey. In Kia Pumau Tonu. *Proceedings of Hui Whakapumau*, Maori Development Conference, Massey University.

Wereta, W. (1994) Maori Demographic Trends. In Kia Pumau Tonu. *Proceedings of Hui Whakapumau*. Maori Development Conference, Massey University.

Wilson, Julius (1987) *The Truly Disadvantaged: The Inner City, The Underclass, and Public Policy*. Chicago IL & London: University of Chicago Press.

Panel Discussion – Family Members' Perspectives on Family Changes

'Mary'

Thank you for this opportunity to speak. I hope you will find this brief excerpt of my life worth hearing about, as it summarises what have been probably the most important learning opportunities I shall ever have.

I have twice been a step-parent, and twice a single parent. I was married at the age of 22 to a widower with two small sons, then aged 7 and 8 – and so I became a step-parent knowing absolutely nothing about parenting, let alone step-parenting. In some ways this may have been a good thing as at least I wasn't constantly making comparisons. In actual fact, I found step-parenting then – and later – really quite easy – it was the difficulties and hassles around the relationships with my partners that I found difficult!!

In addition to the two boys, we then had three children . . . and for some time life was fine – I had always wanted a large family – and I had it. I was working as well, and so life was pretty busy, but satisfying mostly.

However, life being what it is, it didn't stay fine and over a period of years I came to realise that this was a most unsatisfactory relationship. And so began a long, sad process toward separation.

After some time I 'repartnered' and lived with a man who had been married twice before. His two daughters from his first marriage lived with us, and a son from the second marriage who was in Australia visited for holidays three times a year – an expensive and traumatic process, but wonderful when he got there!

Sadly – very sadly for me and my children, as we were mostly very happy – my defacto partner continued his old patterns and within five years had found the next love of his life . . . and so soon my children and I were once again a single-parent family – although a very different one to the first time.

I often look back and wonder how much of the 'breakdown' of these relationships was caused by step-parenting/step-family factors. However, I always see other factors as being more the cause – mostly my partner!! – but not the difficulties of step-parenting.

When I look back, I still believe that the children were all generally very happy – and my children assure me that this was so for them. They were all teenagers, and so life definitely had its ups and downs for us all – but they were all pretty mild compared with the strife that some families have. Because I am not them, I know that I cannot really know for sure that it was a happy arrangement for all of them, but I do know that they all did really well at school – they were academically high achievers, and they all had busy and positive social and sporting lives – and there was a lot of fun and positive interaction amongst us all at home. One of my step-daughters chose to isolate herself a lot, and that was difficult for us sometimes, but it was also pretty 'normal' teenage behaviour – and legitimate if that was what she needed to do. However, for whatever reason, my partner's needs were elsewhere, and sadly, as he withdrew, his children also withdrew; their loyalty was naturally to him. And my children grouped around me, and suddenly there was a huge division between the two families which was eventually unable to be crossed. In retrospect there were many possible reasons for this, but the obvious message is that if the parents are not one hundred percent committed to each other, the rest of the unit is likely to collapse fairly quickly. And it did. I think that the difficulties that the children experienced were exacerbated and 'used' to feed my partners fears and inadequacies – and so fuel his need – for whatever reason – to move on.

However, again I want to stress that generally my experience – and my children's – of this step-family was really positive. In fact it was mostly an absolute joy – there was so much enjoyment and satisfaction – as well as challenge – in the interactions within our household, as well as the interactions with our other families . . . it was not all stress by any means! My children developed really close bonds with their step-sisters and step-brother, and their step-father too. We all experienced this big and busy family as an exciting and joyful place to be – and still feel we were very lucky to have had this experience.

None-the-less there were things about step-families that were very difficult, and some of these proved to be so in both the experiences I had – and so I would like to talk about these – and in particular those which were difficult for the children. And I will briefly compare step-families with single parent families, and then share some of what I have learned.

The greatest difficulties – both for the children and for me – were around the impact of the step-children's non custodial parent – and grandparents, and new family . . . issues of justice and fairness over material things like Christmas presents, monetary and other gifts, holidays, etc. – my children 'suffered' from a father who was far less generous – and maybe less able to be generous – than their step-siblings' mother. Similarly they felt emotionally less 'wanted' by their father than their step-siblings – rightly or wrongly, this was their perception. The needs of the other family also created difficulties – juggling our holidays around the other families – and in my second relationship there were three other families to consider – was difficult to say the least – and often resulted in one set of children feeling that their needs and those of their 'other' parent had not been fully met. It also of course created situations where the children felt their other parent was considered a nuisance – no matter how hard we tried to ensure that this did not happen.

Inherent in the difficulties with the 'other' family were issues around secrecy – plans, activities, and information being withheld – and eventually it became clear that this was being sanctioned by my partner, partly perhaps because he felt this was what his daughters needed or wanted – but largely I felt as a power issue. There is a fine line in step-families between each family retaining its separate identity, and the need for these two families to operate as one . . . both are important, but it is hard for both to happen unless there is open communication – no secrets, no withholding of information – at least as far as possible.

Another area of difficulty was the level of competitiveness between some of the children – particularly two of them (one from each family, both girls). Whilst this was difficult, it was also completely 'normal'. I tried to take the view that they would grow out of it, but my partner was unable to live with this and it grew to be a major issue for us as parents – which of course made it even more difficult for the children. Protectiveness and defensiveness are very destructive in a step-family.

The greatest difficulty for my children was to come – the single parent environment was much more difficult for them, for a variety of reasons. Of course, I acknowledge that our experience of a single parent family is not the 'norm' and I am aware that for many children the single parent family environment is a very positive one. Ours was not – because of the way in which it came about. After a very happy and warm, loving open relationship between both families and especially my partner and I, there was a complete shift in his behaviour. The reasons later became clear, but at the time there was no apparent reason at all.

His children mirrored his behaviour – as might be expected in close families – and the split between the two families became huge – and yet neither the children nor I understood why.

Thus the separation when it came was bitter and painful for all of us – except of course my partner who had another relationship to go to. My children and I were all devastated, confused, enormously hurt and had little faith in anyone. I was not in a good emotional state – and I was, for a while, an appalling parent – I was inconsistent, unreasonable and irrational. I had huge anxiety and panic attacks, together with guilt, rage and helplessness. In addition to having to 'cope' with me, my children were experiencing their own pain and anguish, and were much in need of support and stability which I was unable to give. They felt betrayed, rejected and humiliated. They experienced guilt, rage, hurt, and confusion in an ongoing way for months, and in a milder form for years. The loss was enormous – not only the person they had come to love as their father, but a whole family, their sisters and brother – and, for the second time, their home. It was a very difficult time for them – far more difficult than the first experience of single parent family life.

One of the factors which made this second separation particularly difficult was that my ex-partner refused to have any contact with my children, or allow them – or me – to have contact with his children. He refused to give reasons for this, although when his next new family moved into 'our' house very soon after we left, the reason became obvious. This total and complete separation was extremely hard for us all. It seemed essential that he was part of the healing process by at least hearing and acknowledging our anger and pain – the fact that he seemed to be totally oblivious to it made it much worse for us.

Apart from the difficulties peculiar to that particular situation, there was an interesting other phenomenon which we had experienced the first time, and which was very obvious again the second time, and that is the lack of status for single parent families. As a single parent, I always felt inferior, somehow socially deficient. However, as a step-parent I felt I was very much admired and highly regarded – a very different situation. My children were also very aware of this difference, especially the second time.

So what have I learned from all of this?

I have learned that the one hundred percent commitment of the adults to each other is essential and central. Obviously no-one wants a relationship that is bad for the children. Without total commitment to each other, there is no stability for the children and the unit really doesn't stand a chance.

I have learned the importance of recognising and acknowledging the effects of adult decisions and behaviours for the children. I see that they are all too often dismissed, or not given enough consideration. I don't suggest that separation is not OK, but the way in which it is done is hugely important. Honesty with children is paramount.

On-going contact – or at least the option of it – is important, especially for the children. Children need to be able to decide for themselves how they will continue to relate to an absent parent – if at all – but the option should be there. I think that this is particularly important in the case of step-parents as often the children have been expected to make enormous adjustments for the sake of the step-family, and on-going contact is an important way of acknowledging their contribution – as well as assuring them that they are not being blamed for the separation. I think this is equally important in separation of intact families as well.

I have learned that step-families can be very happy and exciting places to be! And that both children and adults have the opportunity to learn some very valuable life skills in the process of the ups and downs!

And I have learned that parenting, whether on one's own or with a partner, although difficult, is an enormously rewarding job – but it needs to be viewed as a positive and valuable experience, not as a 'nuisance' or something that can easily be walked away from. It is not OK to just 'dump' children in order to get oneself a better life.

Perhaps the most important learning is that adults need to get their act together in their relationships and behave more responsibly for the children – both in intact families and in step-families. I think that adults getting into relationships tend to forget the effects their behaviours may have on the children.

The commitment to the children, in intact families, separated families, and step-families, must be taken far more seriously, so that the children's emotional and physical welfare is paramount. And in step-families the commitment must be to the step-children as well as the new partner.

'John'

Greetings everybody.

I'm on the teaching staff at this university. I've been asked to talk about a fairly personal matter. I appreciate the fact that the press is not here and of course I'm happy to share with you some fairly personal things. However, political issues are public knowledge, but private/personal issues are not, of course. They're confidential.

I'm not going to tell you why my marriage broke up. It broke up about ten years ago. The first few years after that time we had custody and access. And then about five years ago it became shared custody. As I say, I'm not going to tell you why the marriage broke up. I think decisions about who one's going to spend one's life with are not one hundred percent rational. And I don't think they should be. Many of us make mistakes and we will continue to make mistakes. I should perhaps say, however, that both my ex wife and I had had quite a turbulent adolescence, with major psychiatric problems. What I want to do is to deal with some of the stages of the healing process. We've been apart for nearly ten years now and my elder daughter is now fifteen, she was six at the time we moved apart. My younger daughter was aged three when we moved apart and it is her twelfth birthday today.

So, first, at the time we moved apart, the one thing I was able to ask my wife and she was able to agree upon, was that we should not use the children as part of our continuing feud. And we agreed to that and have stuck to that. I think it's one of the most important issues to reach an agreement on at the time of separation.

Secondly, our general practitioner recommended us to have some joint counselling sessions and we had four sessions with a very skilled clinical psychologist. This wasn't aimed at trying to patch it up or bring it back together again, but to create a new relationship where both parents can still co-operate in bringing up the children, even though they live in different places. I firmly believe that children need two committed parents. It is a serious human rights issue to deprive one parent of his children. I say this, because I suspect it is usually the father who is deprived, but there are various different viewpoints on that. Now there are all sorts of factors which mitigate against that reconciliation and instead try to maintain and reinforce a state of confrontation. Everyone seems to assume that after a marriage breakdown, confrontation, rather than healing, is a natural state of affairs. For instance, friends. One finds that those who were friends of one partner before the marriage, become enemies of the other partner after a marriage breaks down. Relations. On the Christmas after we separated, which was a difficult time for me, I asked my parents to join me from England to spend Christmas with me and my children. In the course of that, I found myself losing my temper with my parents, because they were taking my side on the issue. Now at that time, I perceived my job was to keep a leaky ship still afloat and anyone who takes sides in that is rocking the boat and it doesn't help. The real help comes from friends and relationships who can maintain contact with both partners. And I'm happy to say that one of my closest friends in New Zealand is the brother of my ex-wife, a minister of religion in the South Island.

Thirdly, professionals called in to help. Now this bit is not from personal experience, but I do know of persons who have experienced marriage breakdown who were sent to psychological counsellors and who came away with the distinct impression that that professional had taken sides against them. In a particular case I'm thinking of, to which I know quite a bit about the background, all I can say is that the separation was intensely sad, but actually no one was to blame. Professional counsellors need to be very careful about this, especially at a time when gender issues are so intense.

Fourthly, our public institutions also habitually assume that confrontation is the natural state of affairs in marriage breakdown. For a period of some years, my ex-wife considered that in the interests of the children, she could not take on full-time work. So she claimed the domestic purposes benefit or the unemployment benefit. And I had to pay the liable parent contribution, child support. Now the documentation from the Department of Social Welfare unmistakably makes the assumption that a state of confrontation exists. It leaves no room for any alternative. I find this offensive. At another stage, my ex-wife needed a house and couldn't afford the full price, so I put up some of the money. Now when it came to child support, I thought that some consideration should be given to this fact to determine how much I paid. I consulted my lawyer and basically, he said, I didn't stand a chance of any compensation. Incidentally, now we're within ten minutes walk of each other which is a very important factor in the success of the new arrangement.

Now for some other less political issues. After the separation, for many years, I experienced very difficult behaviour from the older daughter. It was absolutely infuriating at times, but I didn't know why, at the time. I now interpret this as a combination of sibling rivalry and anger at the fact that her two parents had moved apart. I didn't realise that was the reason at the time, but I do now. This is very difficult to cope with. And that brings me to another point about the potential for violence in a family. A potential which I think is probably worse in single parent families. I won't say much about this. I think anyone who knows me will think I'm an extremely non-violent person, a pathologically non-violent person. But, I do know what it's like to be pushed to the limit. I was wrestling with the turmoil of my own emotions and here was a destructive and hostile child. I am also extremely sensitive to noise and under those circumstances, it's very difficult, especially when the children realise you are sensitive to noise and exploit the fact. So, I ask you, do you know where your own breaking point is? Have you catered for the fact that people differ in the point at which they lose their calm? I personally think it might be better, and I say this to people who are involved in counselling, it might be better to teach people how to lose their temper quickly and relatively mildly rather than bottling it up to the point where it reaches dangerous and explosive proportions. And I learnt that message the hard way. I think on the whole, on this issue of violence within the family, we should perhaps have less moralism and more realism about the circumstances in which it occurs.

I want to finish on a happy note. In the last few years, things have gone very well. My children behave nicely to each other, to me, to their mother. The older one is always volunteering help around the house. We come together for a family meal at Christmas. Both children seem to be shaping up as contented well-balanced adolescents with good senses of humour. It gives me a profound sense of relief after all the trauma experienced by both their parents at these early stages of life. Touch wood. But it is expensive. I earn a senior lecturer's salary. Over the past ten years, I've probably paid between $80,000 and $100,000 as a result of the separation. Some of that is an inevitable part of separation, but some of it is quite unfair I believe. It becomes increasingly difficult to imagine how one could make a success of the new arrangement if you're not earning good money. Well, I don't know what to call this, whether to call it a success story or not. If it is a success story, it is not just me who takes the credit for it. It is all four of us.

'Sarah'

At first I'll start with a little history of me. I'm a 'child' and I'm in my twenties. But I'm still loved and I've got two parents and I've got a step-monster and I've got a step-father. The reason that I don't get on very well with my step-monster is because when I was quite young, my father had an affair with her, which shattered and upset me. Lots of funny things happened along the way and a lot were upsetting and a lot weren't very nice, but I think because I'm quite cynical and quite unpleasant, that I survived.

Basically what I want to say is <u>not</u> that everybody should be blamed. When I was 15, my mother and I moved to x. It was kind of a shock because my mother said only three days before we left, 'you're going to live in x' and I said 'I think I'm not', because I'd lived in y for all my life and I liked y – it was little and comfortable and I was quite a big fish at that stage and it was a bit of a waste to move to x and be a little fish. So, Mum and I came to x and my father said 'let's get back together' and my mother said 'Aaah well, perhaps we could' and we said 'No Mum'. And Mum said 'alright then'. So, she was pretty happy and she'd got up spirits for the first time in probably about a year and she took off to visit him – a surprise visit – and found him in bed with my step-monster. It wasn't very pleasant. The funny thing she did do was get the keys to his Mercedes and drive over to the other side of town, so when he got up in the morning, he couldn't find it and wept many a tear, so that was kind of good.

When she came back, that was kind of when the trouble started. Some doctor had put her on halcyon, so I don't know whether to blame that or not, but at one stage she took an overdose of pills and was quite sick, but didn't die which was very lucky. After that, things were pretty grotty for probably about three years. In my first year at varsity, things were pretty rotten and I decided that I would leave home, but I feel fairly bad about leaving, because I left her by herself, but she was also quite difficult to live with and I was quite sick of hearing that my father was rotten and that she was unhappy and I really wanted to be away from all of that because it was quite difficult.

So what I wanted to tell people was that maybe some good ideas are you've got to tell your children when you separate, although it's very difficult, you've got to let them know that something's going on, not just sort of pretend that everything's rosey. And so what we did, my brothers and I all thought 'Aaah, that horrible mother of ours, she's such a grumpy old woman', but it was really because she knew that my father had been unfaithful and she was just going through the motions. I think a lot of people are expected to do that then, and quite a few wives I think as well. Once I moved and lived with my mother, I think perhaps the problems were that her anger and upset were transferred onto me. For example, if I went out in the weekend with my 16 or 17 year old friends, Mum would say 'be home at 9:30' and my friends would be allowed to be out until 11. And I would go 'Hmmmm' and I wasn't a bad child, so I would go home at 9:30, but it would be another issue. When I got home at, say, 9:35, there would be a huge screaming match, as if I'd set fire to the house and I hadn't and I was quite nice at the time. So I tried to be good but because she was in so much pain, it was a lot easier to push it onto me and make me feel – I know she didn't mean to – but she made me feel like a lot of it was my fault at the time. And so what I think about that is consistency. I know that lots of parenting books say now be consistent with your children and have a bedtime for them at the right time and feed them at this time and yell at them for doing something, but make sure you yell at them next time too. Don't say ' that's a funny joke' one time and then ' don't do it again' the next time. So that's what I found was very difficult. Because it wasn't a very open environment with my parents and because it was a tit for tat kind of 'I hate him', 'I hate her' kind of thing, it ended up that we all just lied to each other and there were lots of lies going around and no-one was really telling anybody how they felt. Everybody just grumped at each other and grumped about each other.

Finally, about a year ago, everybody started pulling themselves together and we've all managed to be a bit more honest and work out what happened. It's almost ten years ago that it started and we didn't find out until five years ago what was going on. And there's a lot of things that we've just come to know and I guess that's because we're grown-ups now. But, we should have been let into a wee bit of the secret, because we just saw our whole house and cats and dogs and pets and family members – all just went 'bang'. Everybody was gone. So, we could have been explained to a little bit more and although you can't just blame anyone – I know everybody worked as hard as they could and we worked hard as well.

One of the things that I've talked about to people who are my age, is that you feel at that time that you are not a murderer and you are not a thief and you are not a horrible person and you haven't been arrested, so why are your parents being hard on you and I think you have to remember that your kids are good.

'Martin'

Thank you for this opportunity to be able to share some things that have affected my life in a big way. It was one thing to have read, studied and practised the counselling of people for many years, and then to find oneself in the middle of such a situation.

I come from the point of view of being a step-father. My wife has access every school holidays with her six-and-a-half year old son.

Interestingly, this past week and preceding weeks, I've been in a series of meetings talking about liberty and freedom of justice. At the close of one meeting the other day, we sang a song, 'Let Justice Flow Down Like A River'. In some respects, from what you'll hear from my story, you would think a dam was in the river.

I shall firstly outline my story with my wife and her little boy with a few headlines. Six lawyers, including Counsel for the Child, three judges, many pre-hearing conferences, one psychologist, two Section 29A reports, one psychotherapist's report and two NZ Children and Young Persons Service investigations. All equity in our home has gone because of legal aid and paying child support out of a student allowance. The little boy's behaviour is sadly affected. His sister keeps asking as each plane flies over our place 'is my brother coming?' And I'm trying to do full-time study. That's some of the headlines.

Still awaiting for an appeal date after two years.

All this has happened in the space of about four years. It came about when my now wife was separated from a pretty sad situation where the family were suffering verbal and emotional abuse, and the oldest daughter (16 years) was being molested. The father, who now has custody, is in his early fifties. He never had any previous relationships and has never had any children.

The first stage in this journey for my wife, was that she went for Family Court counselling. She was told to forgive her husband, to stay with him and if she stayed for thirty years he would probably change. Custody and access arrangements were bulldozed through. The father had access. He was a very stressful man, he dictated what she should be doing and when he came to return the child after an access visit, it wasn't the child who burst out crying, it was the father. This had a detrimental effect on everybody.

My wife's mother was seriously ill and died in that very year. My wife was subject to many anonymous, abusive phone calls. She sought the advice of a lawyer and asked ' can I relocate somewhere else so I can get some calm'. He said, 'Yes, you go. We'll sort out the access arrangements later'. She did go for a holiday for four weeks, for some time out. It was about this time that I was doing some reading on this whole subject. First was a book from Australia, which was called *The Family Court Jungle*. The next was *Mothers on Trial* and the other one was *Men Who Hate Women*. Some of you have probably read them.

My wife went away on a holiday. However, one day, whilst driving down the road at her holiday place, a Policeman stopped her and said 'I want you to come to the Police Station, I have an Ex Parte order for you'. Counsel for the Child rang her up and said 'if you're any sort of mother, you'd bring this little boy back. You have no rights. You have nothing whatsoever, you are only a baby-sitter'. At a later stage he had meetings with the two older children and told them that their mother was stupid and foolish, and shouldn't be doing what she'd done. He never listened to the older children.

It was interesting that as he said all this, a similar case in which he appeared as counsel, resulted in a decision against his client with the Court of Appeal stating the opposite of what he had told my wife and her children, i.e. allowing a custodial parent, a mother, to relocate. He obviously forgot this. He was asked to set up mediation conferences on several occasions. Nothing was done.

The other key person in this whole saga was the psychologist who told us at our initial meeting that she didn't like us very much and we shouldn't be doing what we were doing. We were never interviewed in the home setting. There were certain confidential pieces of information we told the psychologist during our interview, which she then passed on to the father who used it against my wife at the hearing.

In the second report, she made a promise to the little boy, because he kept saying all the time 'I want to talk to the Judge man please'. And she said 'Well, I'm afraid you're not allowed to, but I will tell him what you want'. She didn't, plus a lot of other relevant information was omitted from the Section 29A report.

After many conferences, the Family Court Judge told us, as we were preparing to leave for Dunedin because I was going to take study here, that going to Dunedin would not prejudice the case in any way. During the hearing, my wife and I were severely criticised by the opposing counsel and told that we were stupid to be listening to this sort of advice.

The two older children, during the hearing, were discredited by the Judge, when they explained the type of abuse that they had been under all this time.

Now, my observations. As a counsellor and having heard many, many sad stories over the years, and having clients sitting in front of me crying and talking to me in their childhood voices, I find it very, very difficult to see this little boy going through the same steps, when in fact they could be prevented. For example, some of his behaviours. He is drawing pictures now of taking his pants off and showing his genitals. He also practices this at school. He tries to get behind our dogs and hump them or sits or kneels in front of them. He tries to get his little sister into the bed and tries to get on top of her in bed, on the floor and on an earlier occasion, the bath. He tried to do this with his mother too. He goes to adult women he has never met before and strokes their thighs, caresses their breasts and goes into a strange trance. Every visit, he breaks down and cries. He goes silent when it's time to go home. The last visit he cried and cried for about three hours. He said 'I'm tired of crying, I'm tired of being sad'.

The other aspect in this whole business is finances. Without legal aid of course, it's impossible to have legal counsel and attend hearings. It has come to the point where we can't shift house because we've got no equity left. It also means that our mortgage has increased dramatically. That means we have to pay extra mortgage repayment insurance. If we earn any extra money, then it goes towards paying off legal aid. Then you have Child Support. My wife's only income at the first stage was family support for our little daughter. After this, she had to pay 50 percent of this to Child Support. The question I ask of Inland Revenue and the Child Support Act is, who has a greater right? Which child? Particularly when the father is earning $60,000. Who is supporting the children?

Who is supporting and caring for the children? Who supports this little boy when he is by himself in his bedroom, crying for his mother? He says he is sad all the time at his Dad's place. His mother cared for him with his acute hearing loss and glue ear, and the ensuing operations. His mother cared for him while he was diagnosed as having epilepsy. She left the whole bad environment to protect him from the ongoing trauma and now he's back at the source of it – abandoned, betrayed and neglected.

I've had several children, in the last few months, come to me for help. All have the same sort of scenario. Just a couple of weeks ago, a young fifteen year old, who had attempted suicide because he'd been through this whole sorry saga himself.

So, in summary, being a step-parent, a husband of an access parent with a severely disturbed boy is pretty rough going. It doesn't do a lot for my study. Knowing what has happened to my wife, daughter and step-son, and being a counsellor, causes me great anxiousness. Knowing that the things that should have happened in the family law system haven't. Knowing that the welfare of the child is paramount. Knowing that the time-frame which a child understands should be adhered to also. Lawyers who have said they're experienced in family law and then drop out. A huge number of conflicting opinions. I suppose in summary I could say the system fiddles while a child and a mother burns. How do we cope with this crisis? Well, we sit down and we cry and we share a lot. We encourage one another to have a belief that there is a God who gives strength, help and hope that truth and justice will flow down like a river.

The Legal Realities
for Children and Families –
Part One: 'A Legal Overview'

Mark Henaghan
Faculty of Law, University of Otago

(Transcript of an oral address and discussion)

I thought today I would explore two themes with you and I am quite happy as I go along, because I am going to use a couple of cases to illustrate these themes, for people to put their hand up and discuss issues at a particular moment. It is important that if there is a particular process that you thought was inappropriate in the cases I am talking about, you feel it could have been done better to say so. If there's expertise out here, then don't hesitate to put your hand up and just launch into it. So, you are welcome to do that, I encourage that.

The two themes. The first one is one that I have been preaching, trying to preach for a long time. It is always one that you never quite know how people will see it. I have had an experience with lawyers who have taken it very literally. I still don't think we take enough consideration of the child. I think it is easier said than done to be able to understand the child's view of things. I said to lawyers once at a Counsel for the Child seminar that the child's point of view is not considered enough. Of course, they took it very literally, they wanted to have children in court being cross-examined. And that's not what I mean by understand the child's view of things. But they thought that would be a good, legal way of doing things, to get the children involved in the proceedings. Of course, children are not responsible for the break-up, so we should not suddenly say 'Well, what do you think? It's all up to you now kid. Now make up your mind what you're going to do.' That's not what I mean by the child's view of things. I will explain what I mean by it in a minute. That's the first theme I want to explore. I think if we do try to understand the child's view of things, we are likely to make better decisions throughout the whole legal process. Decisions often go wrong, where the child's view of things has been overlooked or not even considered sometimes. Most of the decision-making as always is the case with children, is made by adults.

I also want to raise with you and explore some of the proposals that are being made and currently being debated both in this country and other countries with regard to changes of the law, changes of legal principle, changes in process, which some people argue may improve the decision-making process and may mean that children end up with a better deal. I think the only way to measure those processes and to ensure that they are working properly is to ask the question 'Would using this principle or this process really improve the quality of life for children?' We'll do that as we go along.

Let's then come back to what I mean by the child's view of things. It's reasonably straight forward. The difficulty is finding out about it. How does this child see their world? Often we, as adults, tend to want children to respond to our way of seeing things. Children have their own way of viewing the world, just like all of us do. So, a child's view must be this child in terms of their world. And, one way of tapping into it I think, is to imagine what it would be like to be this particular child. I think family lawyers have quite good imaginations, people working in this area need to be able to say 'What would it be like for this child in this particular situation?' How would you feel to be in this situation? How would you feel if you had to go through this process? What would it mean to you if you were a seven-year-old and this was going on? Use your imagination. Be able to empathise and understand what may be happening to the child. A simple process, but I think, one that is often not done. For example, I saw it the other day. I was at a sports meeting and I had to bite my tongue watching athletics and the teacher was there cheering for the kids. As they came down the straight and finished forth and fifth, they just sort of wandered off and the teacher never came near them. There was one little boy from this teacher's school who won. The teacher leapt out of the grand stand, knocked people out of the way, jumped up and down, embraced the boy, shook his hand and went back and sat down. I had to bite my tongue, 'They're all trying mate, just some have more ability than others.' The perspective of the other kids must be – 'They cheer until I come down the straight and I don't win – I'm not very important any more'. I felt sick in the stomach. It's a simple example, but it's one where for the kid who has tried hard, doesn't have much ability and gets eighth, you still need someone to say to you 'You did very, very well'. That's the respect anyone needs.

Another way of looking at it is to listen to how the child describes their world in their terms. Again, often children are asked questions which adults want the answers to, like the question, which should never be asked of any child, 'Who do you want to live with when your parents break up?' We may want an answer to that, but to make a child responsible for that is inappropriate. But that doesn't mean, because we don't want to ask that question, that we should leave the child out totally. That's where the problem arises. What it does mean, is we have be able to understand what is important in that child's world. It may well be what is important for that child is friends, school, sporting activities, all those other things which are important to the child. And they can be tapped into without putting the child in that hot seat and say 'Choose between Mum and Dad. Choose which weekend you spend where. Choose who you want to have Christmas dinner with.' They are the wrong things to ask children. I don't think anyone who is sensitive to the process would ask a child to do that. But that does not mean it is not important to work out what is important for the child. What the child may be thinking about in terms of the school holidays, what the child is really looking forward to from their point of view. Then we can build decision-making around that without the child having to be in the hot seat. That's what I mean by the child's view of things. And we'll look at examples in two cases.

There are a number of justifications for emphasis on the child's view of things. First of all, the law requires that the child's welfare is the first and paramount legal consideration, in all decisions about children. And I think that if any decisions were made about our welfare as adults, the first thing we would hope is that someone would at least try to find out what is important for us. They are making a decision about us. I used the example at a Counsel for the Child seminar once, where I said that everyone would make a decision about you, people would get together and decide what was good for you and you wouldn't have any say. You would not be consulted at all. How would you feel about that? Most of them took a deep breath. But, that does happen to children quite often. Well-meaning people make decisions without even considering what is going on with the child. I think if children are going to be given equal respect and dignity as human beings, it requires serious consideration of the child's view of what is best for them in terms of their way of seeing the world. It goes back to my original proposition. Not best for them in terms of the question we ask them, but best in terms of the way they see the world. It doesn't mean their view will be necessarily always be followed. We'll look at this as we come to examples. But it should at least be considered, and be considered seriously. Article 12 of the United Nations Convention on the Rights of the Child makes it very clear since 1993 that we are required, being a party to that convention, to consult children in all matters when they are capable of forming views. They have a right to express views freely and weight should be given according to their age and maturity. Article 12 is really an enshrinement of what we already have in our legislation in section 23 of the Guardianship Act, which says in custody and access matters, the views of the child shall be ascertained and given weight according to age and maturity. So it's in the law. It is not as if the law doesn't require the child's point of view. It is just that we have difficulties in being able to do it appropriately. These cases will bring that out. Psychologically, it works. One of the best books I've ever read on being a parent is by Bruno Betelheim called 'A Good Enough Parent'. The one key thing he said in there, which I have found quite helpful in working with my own children and anyone's children really, is the parents' most important task is to get a feeling of what things may mean to the child and handle things in a way that are most helpful to both. I think that when you do get a frustrated or a problem child, you must understand what is going on for them and not just react how you want them to be. There is normally a reason for why they are acting that way, if you understand that, things can work out for both. We were all children once and know what it felt like to us to be in a powerless position with someone doing something that didn't work.

Let's look at these cases. As lawyers, we only really can understand the world through cases. These are both actual cases. We'll look at two. They have gone to court and I think they raise probably all the issues one needs to look at with regard to how the legal process works with children and their families. Both were decided in the North Island.

The first case is about a little boy who was actually called 'Solo', rather appropriate. Let's go right back to Solo's beginnings. His Mum and Dad were engaged to be married, but they did not actually get married. The mother got pregnant and did not want to have Solo right from the beginning. The engagement fell off and Dad drifted off for a period. At the moment of birth, they were living together. So at the moment of birth, an important thing happened legally. The law says certain things when a child is born. Section 6 of the Guardianship Act is a very important provision. When a child is born to a couple, whether they are married or not, if they are living together at the time of the birth, they both become in law what is called legal guardians of that child. Both of them have that right, right from the moment of birth. Which means, legally, that they both have a right to control the child, Solo's, upbringing and they both have a right to physically care for Solo. Some say that this guardianship concept gives parents right from the beginning, the wrong messages – that the child is your possession to do something with. It's your right to control it. It's your right to have physical care of it. That's why people fight over it, because they are given possessionary messages by the law right from the very beginning. But, I think there are good reasons why we have to give rights to parents. They don't have to necessarily be interpreted as being possessionary.

First of all, look at it from Solo's point of view. When he is born, he is pretty helpless. He needs someone who wants to take some responsibility for him. He is not going to be able to do it on his own. Parents have duties to nurture and bring up their children, to make sure they grow up to be healthy human beings. Because they have that duty and responsibility, they have to have a right to control the upbringing, because you cannot do one without the other. It also gives parents a right with regard to the outside world. Other people cannot just come in and start telling you how to bring up your child, although it might be useful in some situations, unless they can show that you are not exercising your right appropriately.

So what happened here was, Dad drifted off after the engagement, the relationship broke up. He still had the right to control, but he gave up his right to physical care. Mum looked after him. Mum entered into a new relationship. When Solo was four, Mum got engaged to another man, and had another child to him. Dad still maintained some contact. Mum's relationship fell apart and when Solo was six, Mum entered a relationship with another man who she married and had a child to him. Both these little children were, half-sisters to Solo. That relationship went really wrong and in fact, the mother had to flee from that relationship from Napier to Whangarei to escape. Solo, in three years, went to four different schools.

Dad in the meantime, went down to Wellington, got a steady job and re-married. He married a nurse called Celia. Dad and the nurse are happily married, but Dad did not have any more children. He had a medical problem and could not have any more children. He was settled in a stable, family relationship down in Wellington and they want Solo to come and live with them during the school year, because they think they will do a better job than Solo living with his Mum. Mum is living with her parents in Napier. She had this period of different relationships which hadn't work. She has now settled down with her parents living in Napier, living in their house. Mum's parents are going to go to Christchurch and will leave her in their house, in Napier. But, Dad and Celia want Solo in Wellington.

Let's then look at the processes that would be available to them to sort this out and see what actually happens. You may be surprised to see what happened in this case.

All parties could go to a counselling session where they could try and work out whether Solo should spend the school year in Wellington which is one option and the holidays in Napier, or whether or not Dad and Celia would move from Wellington to Napier.

Many people misunderstand counselling and I know Judge Blaikie will talk about this. It is not there for therapeutic purposes. That is not the primary reason. It is part of the legal process under the Family Proceedings Act. It is there to resolve a situation and give people the opportunity to discuss options. They might want therapeutic counselling, that's available separately, but not necessarily strictly through the Family Court. My major concern, is I hope that during this process that children's views are considered too. There is nothing in the law re- quiring them to be considered during the counselling process. But I would as- sume good counselling would mean that they would say 'Have you considered how the child is going to cope with this?' Say, for example, they agree and Solo does not want to go. He is happy at school. Say that this is the scenario. Mum thinks Dad's going to fight this right to the end for example. And he's going to keep going and coming at me. I just don't have the energy to keep fighting him off. I think it is easier in some ways to send him off to Wellington to school for a while. That'll get Dad of my back for a while, hopefully Solo will cope with it, not that he is that happy about it, but he will cope with it and I can at least look after my daughters and I won't have to go through a lot of legal proceedings. And that is a common sense view, perhaps, to take.

There is nothing legally stopping them agreeing to this. Yet, apart from the counsellor perhaps saying 'Look, have you really thought this through for Solo?' there is no one necessarily protecting whether the agreement is going to work for the child. If it goes to court, then there are the protections of Counsel for the Child. Unless the child really does cope very badly in Wellington and then it may be a Children and Young Persons issue. But the assumption is that no matter how unhappy the parents may make the child, there is no real check there, which I have some concerns about. We should have some checks built into the system at that stage to ensure that people aren't making decisions which are inappropriate be- cause they just want to get the matter out of the way and the don't want to have to face perhaps long legal proceedings. At least in mediation, a Judge is present. Now again, there is no requirement in a mediation conference that the child is to be considered. Sometimes Counsel for the Child are appointed, and sometimes they are not at this particular stage. One would hope that at a mediation confer- ence when a consent order is made, everyone does say 'Now, how is this going to work for Solo?', 'Is Solo going to be able to cope with this?', 'Has anyone thought how much of a trauma it may be?', 'How are we going to cope with the trauma?'. Counselling and mediation did not work in Solo's case, the mother went to Court.

The 29A reporter said 'He is settled at school. Leave him with his mother. He has not been very happy. He has now reached a point where he is doing quite well. I think we should leave him where he is.' Again, I am still not sure whether the Section 29A reporter had really thought 'Is it important for Solo to be where he is, at that school, or is it more important for him to be, in his mind, somewhere else or see more of his father or whatever?' What seemed to be important here was that he was settled at school, in other words leave things as they are, that's a good psychological thing to do. Section 29A reporters are primarily there to report on the child. But I think sometimes Section 29A reporters, either by the system or by their own perceptions of the system, feel they are there somehow to decide who is the better parent. This is part of what they obviously are doing. But, primarily, they are required to report on the child, to bring out what is important for the child, not necessarily who is better between Mum and Dad. That is part of what they do, but I argue that should be secondary. The report is on the child. That must be the central focus of the report in my view. But often, the court is in a situation where it has to decide between these two people, so you are brought into a situation where you feel well, that's fine, you talk about the parents, but you can't separate them out from the child. My concern is you must also talk about what is going on for the child. I would hope that is a mandatory part of a Section 29A report. What has happened to the child, how does the child cope with what is going on, what is important for this child. That should be part of the report, as well as comment on the parenting skills.

Counsel for the Child at this stage, also felt maintaining current stability was crucial, and it is not clear again from this case, whether that was Solo's view. So, at this stage, what do you think is going to happen to Solo then?

Let's go through the decision. Now we go to the next part of the process. This is the part where people either get concerned or not. We go to a very important part of the legal process. A judge had the discretion here. And that discretion will be exercised, I think it is important for everyone to know, largely on the basis of the values the judge thinks are important. Because welfare is not defined in the Act, the judge has to pick out what values the judge thinks are important. And also, on the judge's perception, that's all the judge has got to go on, of these people. Here's how the judge, in the judge's own words and I won't say whether it was a male or female judge, saw it.

Here's the mother: 'She is a person who encourages reading and creativity.' There was a social work report done on Solo and it said that Solo had impressive development due to his mother. Now there was also a negative side against the mother, which was touched upon in the judgement, which I think is important, it was that after the child was born in the early years, she did over-discipline him. She was quite severe on the discipline of him and she admitted that in evidence. There was a strong emotional bond between the mother and Solo. But he was described as having impressive development and now that he was settled in at school, was doing quite well. 'She has a strong emphasis on education.' So those are quite good points, depending on your values. She has brought him up for the last eight years and he is doing well. But in the judge's view, there were two major weaknesses. One was lack of material security, according to the judge in this case. The lack of material security being that she was on the benefit, which I would have thought is material security – the benefit is there, but in other words her material security was not as good as the father's, where both parties were working. She was on her own with three kids, coping on the benefit. And the one that did seem to be looked at against her, was that she lacked the sense of the realities of life! What it meant was that she had moved in and out a number of relationships which had been tough for her and for the child. She'd been in three different relationships and hadn't quite settled down. So in this judge's perception, that was not a good thing.

Now the father, how was the father described? 'He was stable, emotionally and materially.' Very stable and not only was he stable emotionally and materially, he had a partner who was firm, and who would guide Solo, and there would be team work between Celia and the father. So that was important.

So here we go. He said 'Look, both of your are impressive, you are really impressive. But, I have got to decide where does Solo live – Wellington for the school year or Napier? Here is the decision, we will just go through it – the Judge said 'It is easier for Solo to move to Wellington and go to school there, than have his father move to Napier.' The Judge said 'It is easier for Solo to move, Dad's got a job and Celia has got a job. It is hard for them to uplift and come to Napier.' Solo is just a little kid and he can hop on a train and go down there no problems at all. And this is where the child's point of view has really been left out. 'If Solo only visited the father during school holidays, the father would hardly see him. He would be working at night.' And here's the one – this is quite important – the Judge thought 'He needs a male figure in his life.' 'He needs the stability and a natural family environment', which I think means living with a couple who are married, not with a solo parent. So the decision was made and the judge was very careful to say 'I do not want to have winners and losers here', but we know who was losing and who was winning at this stage. 'I am not going to make a custody order. I am going to make a guardianship order and he will attend school in Wellington and he will spend the school holidays in Napier.' And he said 'That's the guardianship direction I am making and I hope it will work perfectly well.' and the child had to go off. Now what do you think happened as an outcome? Just step back for a minute and think of Solo's point of view. If you were Solo, what do you think? I've been living in Napier, I have been up and down the country, but I am settling into school. How would you feel?

'Pissed off.'

How do you think Celia and Dad are going to cope, when they have never had a child in their life?

'Won't cope.'

That's right. They didn't cope.

What happened was, he went off there, but after the August school holidays when he came back to Napier, he said 'I'm going to stay exactly where I am'. And the family in Wellington were not functioning very well, mainly because they were treating Solo as an older child and they expected more of him, because they wanted the child, but expected him to be older. Mum made a mistake, and this was Mum's major mistake of writing a letter which was given in evidence in court. 'For your Dad and Celia to read, Solo. Show this to your lawyer, arse hole. To the two pair of eyes who always but into Solo's letter, how bloody rude, suspicious, and despicable is your invasion of Solo's privacy. Never read your letters you arse hole, jerk.' So it goes on and on. 'He's an individual who is entitled to his own space, that can be seen by your arse hole attitude. He's just a thing. Your possession, you creeps.'

So, it went back to court, because Dad wants Solo back in Wellington and Solo is saying 'I'm not coming back' and Mum is saying 'You stay with me.' What do you do in that situation? Now a psychologist's report was produced for the Court which said that there was a possibility that Solo was too emotionally dependant on the mother and that showed a kind of psychological abuse. He was too dependent on his mother, the relationship was unhealthy. He was too tuned in to his mother.

The judge felt after reading the letter that there was so much animosity, that all access to the mother should be suspended. Solo was to go back to Wellington with no access to Mum.

Now I have this on good authority, where do you think Solo did end up?

Boarding school. Best place for a child like Solo. He ended up solo, on his own.

Now let's go back. Could this case have been done differently or better? Now here are some of the things people think we should do to try and improve the system. I don't know if any of them would have made any difference. First of all, it is argued we should remove the labels of custody and access. Well that was done in this case anyway and it didn't make any difference to the animosity. In England they have parental responsibility orders, they have residence orders, contact orders and in Australia they are moving towards parenting plans. So even though the judge makes an order, it is finally a parent agreements defining who does what. So people don't go out of it thinking 'I won the kid, you lost the kid'. Now there is some strength in that. The judge here, to be fair, tried to do that. If you read the judgement, he did everything possible to try and say 'Look, you are both involved.' When you are living in different districts, there is always going to be more time with one than the other. So, one is going to perceive themselves as the loser. That is what happened here. The other idea, which has been suggested and strongly suggested, is the idea of the primary caregiver presumption. Now people see this as the classic case for that. The idea is, we shouldn't give these judges, especially the male ones, discretion. That is the politically correct view. We should not give these judges discretion, because look what they do. They are only interested in pushing the male point of view. 'This boy needs his father.' Take away the discretion. This has been suggested strongly by the Justice Department, so it is going to keep coming up. The strengths of it are, that first of all, it gets rid of psychologists. That is one of its great strengths. It saves a lot of money, no more 29A reports. Because what you have to do for a primary caregiver presumption is look at who did what tasks. Now the tasks would be the cooking, cleaning and looking after the child. The one who does most of those, leading up to the hearing gets custody. Simple as that. In other words, you've done most of the work, you get custody. As simple as that. Just get neighbours, friends to say who did most of what. It also means the judge cannot focus on the Judge's own values.

'That looks at quantity, not quality.'

It does tend to look at quantity. Yes. And the funny thing that has happened in America where it is being used, is men actually get double the amount for things they do. If they do the dishes, it counts like they do it for a week. They wash a plate one night. 'Yes, I saw him washing a plate through the window. He's been very good.' So it seems that men get a lot of credit for things they don't do much of. 'I saw him putting a peg on the line. I actually saw a guy putting a peg on the line.' So he gets the credit for six months for doing that. The argument is that it protects the primary caregiver. In this case, the assumption would be that Mum has been the primary caregiver – end of case – the child stays with Mum. However, as in law, there are always exceptions and this is where the case would have gone. Unless the primary caregiver is unfit. That is the exception. Now what would have happened in this case is Dad would have argued his case on the basis of what? She 'lacks the sense of realities of life' to put it in the judge's terms. Mucks around, marries three people, can't settle down, bad for Solo. And so that would have been how the case would be argued and the judge would have had just as much reason to say, 'Yes, the male figure is more stable.' And my real worry is that it doesn't mention at all the child's point of view. So while it might tie judges down, I think we are still better on balance to trust the judges. My worry about this is, it switches the focus around to quantity things,, as you've said, who has done what and if you read the judgements in the United States, the child is virtually not mentioned. It is a totting up exercise. All the judge has to do is tick the boxes. How many dishes, how many nappies, how many this, how many that. And at the end of the day, that is who gets custody. It still doesn't help with access, which is the most difficult decision. We look at it in the next case.

So I would say, I am not convinced it is a good way to go. I think the weakness in this case was nobody really looked at Solo's point of view. It was obvious from his point of view, where he wanted to be. And if you are going to reject where he wants to be in Napier, you have to have a good reason for it, moving him down to Wellington, apart from the fact that it is hard for Dad to go up to Napier. That's not a good reason. So I would have thought more consideration for Solo's point of view may have worked there.

We are going to turn now to an access case. This is one that will cause a lot of concern, because it's an issue of the moment and it's a big issue for the court. Another really important concern is the issue of violence.

Here's the children. We've got some very young children, Alesha, Salotte, Rex and Mum and Dad. They were a married couple and they have broken up. There was a consent arrangement for Dad to have access, which shows these consent orders can be made in unusual situations. And it was not happening, because Mum did not want him to have access. The scenario is not uncommon. So Dad, as he is entitled to by law, applied to the court to enforce it. 'I want access to my children. You have agreed to it and I want to see my children.' Access is not defined in the law. All it says is 'a parent can apply for access to their child.' Access can be set with any conditions the court sees appropriate, so a judge, for example, can give access on conditions that you do such and such, or that you see the child in certain situations. Here it was agreed to.

The reason for the mother saying 'I don't want it anymore' was that she alleged specific incidents of violence against her by the father, although she acknowledged he is good with the children. This is your difficult case. A man who is violent towards his wife, but who is good with the children. These are difficult cases and I am sure there will be different points of view out here. And I won't say what the sex of the judge was in this case. You can guess. Not that that should matter.

So let's go through it. Here's what Mum alleged, because again they were serious allegations. There was some supporting evidence and it is important in this case for anyone working in these areas to make sure you do have good evidence. Because while you may believe the person, judges have to be fair to both sides. They have to have evidence. People say 'I didn't like that judge, he didn't seem to believe me.' Well, credibility is something the judge has to weigh up and also the judge has to have evidence of things.

So, first of all, the mother alleged she had been assaulted and he had attempted to stab her. And when she was stabbed, she alleged his family had stopped her going to the doctor, so she could not get that medical evidence. Which, I am sure does happen in some situations. She was frightened, he had said to her 'Look, you go to the doctor and it'll be worse.' And I am sure that does happen, and people who work in refuge will know, people don't go to the doctor when they should and therefore, get the evidence. She did have a dentist certificate stating there was a massive blow to her face, which the dentist said it must have been a massive blow to do that much damage to the teeth. So she had that to back her up. She also had evidence of a psychotherapist who said she was traumatised to the point that her level of functioning was severely reduced. So that's her evidence.

The father denies it all and says 'Once or twice, I pushed her around.' The common scenario, we are used to. 'I didn't stab her, I didn't punch her.' All you've got is a dentist's evidence to say that.

Now the judge, in this case, accepted the Mum's evidence, the dentist's certificate. Even though that is hearsay, strictly speaking. The dentist was not cross-examined and asked about it, just a certificate saying it. The judge was prepared to accept it. In any other court, in a criminal court, it would not even wash. In the family court, they will accept hearsay evidence, because the court can accept any evidence it thinks fit. And also, the judge again, had a perception that the mother was credible as a person, the way she was giving her evidence, and she was very upset about having to give the evidence, and upset about the implications for the wider family.

Now the decision of the judge. What would you do in that case. Would you say 'Well, this is a case where he was a good father.'? And the mother didn't deny that. These children may very well value the relationship with that father. We don't know, the children's perception, it is not mentioned at all. What is discussed is that access was to be stopped not for months, but for years, for the mother to recover. The judge said 'I will stop access, not for months, but for some years. The mother needs to recover from what she has been through.' Three reasons were given by the judge. First of all, safety of the children. The judge, even though there has been no violence against the children at all, thought it could happen. This is the approach of the Domestic Violence Bill that says that anyone who has used violence against a partner, before they will obtain unsupervised access to their children, have to show that they will be safe with the children.

Now one could argue that somebody who has been violent to x, there is always a possibility that they could be violent to y. In the sexual abuse area, we have a risk of abuse. So there could be a risk to these children that he gets angry, he might use violence against them.

The second reason was role-modelling. I find that a little bit difficult, because the couple are not living together. Maybe if the father has another relationship the children will see it through the other relationships. There is also the possibility of seeing it during access handover.

And perhaps the most important reason, and maybe the most convincing one for me here, was the mother's fragility. That she had such a fear of the father, to hand the children over to him, it would affect her functioning as a mother. She would not be able to function as a mother and therefore, their primary caregiver would be at risk.

But what if the children really want to see their father? How do we justify the decision to the children? Because the Domestic Violence Bill says that if you have used violence against your partner, you will get no custody for sure, but you will get at least supervised access. You won't get unsupervised access. Should these children have at least got supervised access or is it better to say 'Look, cut them off altogether', even though it may be important to them? I think this is something people need to think about. First of all Mum has to feel that the children are safe, but also that she is safe from him. Mum's safety is a concern, even with supervised access. If she has to go along to a supervised access centre and drop them off there, he could be lurking around, she is not safe. The real issue here, and we have got to keep the children in mind, is keeping her safe from him and so that if there is going to be dropping off and picking up of children, she should not be anywhere near him at all, because she is going to be terrified of him. So we have to protect her. I fundamentally agree with that. Just saying, 'Go and drop off the kids at supervised access centre', she could easily get assaulted as she comes out the door. So the first thing is that supervised access may be the answer, but not for her to drop them off, for an arrangement to be made whereby a person picks up the children so she is kept safe, and drops them off. But then with supervised access, you just wonder how long does that go on for?

If you fear someone, even in supervised access, she is going to think how do you know they are going to be watching all the time. I fear what he may do, just to get back at me, in that situation. So what do we do? The kids desperately want to see their Dad, because he's a good father remember. Do we say, 'Look, we don't run the risk here.'? Or do we put all the safety checks in place and run the risk. The judge in this case says 'No, we stop it altogether for a number of years.' Do you think the judge was male or female?

'*Female.*'

You're right. Should that have made a difference?

'*No.*'

Not necessarily. Because she actually cited a male judge's judgement to make this decision. So it doesn't make any difference really.

My view is that I think it is important if the children want to see their father, because, ultimately, their welfare is important. And I have a worry with this new Bill, that children could be denied to see their parents. My view is that they should be able to see them, but my view is also that mother must be absolutely made safe and she should not have to drop off the kids and be allowed to be in a situation where she is going to be confronted by the father. And if we took the kids' point of view into it, that he is a good father, they would want to see him. Otherwise, they are going to grow up with this great gap and possibly this view of this great monster.

'*One of the things that comes out of this to me is that with the children, is that three years for the two-year-old is a lifetime-and-a-half and for the eight-year-old, it is a piece of time that is also terribly difficult for an eight-year-old to understand but is more manageable. The child's perception of time seems like forever.*'

I agree. Don't get me wrong. Both these judges who I won't mention, I think are very good judges. None of this stuff is easy.

'*You talked about the newly proposed bill. Could you explain what that is?*'

Yes. Are you not aware of that? Oh, sorry. I have an overhead here. Domestic Violence Bill. It covers more than just custody and access. It covers changes to the whole approach to domestic violence. It widens the net, for example, a number of people, not just people in relationships, people living in flats and other people can apply for orders, it lessens the discretion of giving these orders, it widens the definition of violence to include psychological things, not just physical things and one provision puts in a presumption in custody and access cases that if there is evidence that someone has used violence, and violence in those sections is defined as sexual or physical violence, in the relationship, it could be man against woman or woman against man, then they are not to get custody or unsupervised access unless the court is convinced that they are safe with the children. And there are a number of considerations the court has to consider to measure their safety. Some people have a concern as to whether or not you can ever overcome that burden and that children may miss out on seeing parents. I think the idea behind it is a good one, to protect the custodial parent and the children. It's just that you don't want to go to the point where children start to miss out because we've gone down another track without considering, as you said, the child's perception of these things. The projection is, in March of next year it will come into force. It will require a lot more supervised access centres, it will require a lot of funding for these sort of processes. If children have been in a violent relationship, there will be a lot of trauma there, they will require counselling, which at the moment, apart from the Children, Young Persons and their Families Act, there is not a lot of provision for children who have been in the 'Once Were Warriors' situation, where they have been hiding under the beds, to make sure their trauma of going through it has been dealt with. I know Women's Refuge do an excellent job of counselling, but not every case goes there.

'It concerns me that if the father is seen to be a good father, in terms of the children's point of view, that they would see that to be a good father is to beat up the mother.'

That's a role modelling argument. In other words, if they are exposed to him, is that reinforcing his behaviour as being alright.

'What about the impact of hearing and seeing that violence on the children, not just on the role model.'

Sure, they would have seen that or heard that. But, this came home to me just recently. A person I know very well, revealed to me that his father had been very violent to his mother. He had been rushed away a number of times, driven out of the house. He obviously witnessed that and he is obviously very anti-violence because of it. In a sense he has been traumatised by it, but do we then deny him a relationship with the father who has other qualities, which have been very beneficial to him and he seems to have rejected the violence side, but the other sides have been very beneficial.

'I'm not talking about contact, I'm talking about the meaning – I just have a concern that being a good father does not involve looking after the mother, that being a good father could be that you can beat up the mother.'

I suppose people can be a good father and a terrible spouse, terrible partner.

'I agree with Ruth Busch, who says that spouse abuse is a significant form of child abuse. And from talking to children, I would agree with that. So it's including that idea when working with those men and to qualify that term that to be a good father, they have to include some of those other behaviours in there. I'm not saying this person has not acted as a good father, so they are never allowed to see the children.'

No. You protect your children from things which are abusive to them.

'Yeah. And that might mean that you have some work to do in the relationship to make it better.'

I agree with that. What you are saying is that you should not just look at the father's behaviour with the children, but also behaviour to others which will definitely impact on the child, and will traumatise the child quite deeply, which the situation probably would have done if the children had witnessed it or heard it in some way. Yes, it's a very good point.

'Could I make just one quick point? What worries me, is the assumption that the judge's order on custody and access is going to make that woman safe.'

Yes, I agree. I don't think it makes her safe.

'It might make him a lot more unstable. And this is the problem about supervised access.'

This is the threats of violence argument, the question is what do we do? Do we give in to that or do we say 'That's a court order mate. You disagree with it, you're in the slammer.'

'But, court orders don't work.'

Well, if they don't, they're in contempt of court. They're in the slammer.

'Exactly, but they've got nothing else to lose, when it comes to access with their children they are likely to go a bit further.'

And do some harm.

'Yes.'

That's to hang the sword over the head argument all the time and they get what they want. They just keeping hanging that sword all the time and we always give in to them. So we have two choices, to give in to them and give them what they want, which may not necessarily always be good for the children, or strictly enforce Court orders by Contempt of Court proceedings.

The Legal Realities for Children and Families – Part Two: 'Economic and Property Consequences for Children'

'But Mum! I desperately need the Reeboks'

Annis Eve Somerville
Barrister and Solicitor

Introduction

When a marriage breaks up and there are children, often the custodial parent who cares for the children will be the parent who has been the non-earner or the small earner in the family. The only income the custodial parent often receives is the Domestic Purposes Benefit (DPB). Approximately three quarters of Domestic Purposes Beneficiaries are non-earning parents caring for the children after a break-up of marriage or de facto relationship.

Solo parent families with pre-school children are most likely to be in the bottom income bracket for families with pre-school children. Seven out of ten children living with a sole parent, who is either unemployed or not in the labour force, are in the lowest income bracket. Other statistics reinforce the fact that the non-earner's standard of living drops in the first year after separation. In Australia, unlike New Zealand, women who are the custodial parent are more likely to receive more than 50 percent of the basic matrimonial property assets, usually around 60 percent/40 percent division in their favour.

The average time a beneficiary custodian receives the solo parent benefit is four years. There is no doubt that the children who are cared for by the custodial parent who is a non-earner or a beneficiary are disadvantaged financially. Lenore Weitzman is often quoted from her article, 'The Divorce Revolution', where she stated 'Divorced men experience an average 42 percent **rise** in their standard of living while divorced women and **their children** experience a 73 percent **decline** in the first year after divorce.

Accommodation/Housing

If the custodial parent applies to the Court for an Occupation Order seeking to stay in the family home until the child is 16 years, he/she will not be successful. Unfortunately it is a common myth that the family home will be available until the youngest child reaches the age of 16. However, the custodial parent is usually faced with 'clean break principle', which is the settlement of outstanding issues in relation to matrimonial property, as soon as possible and this often leads to a sale of property. There has been criticism of this principle and that the Act's adherence to the 'clean break principle' undoubtedly over-rides the needs of the children to be properly re-housed. Even if an Occupation Order is granted by the Court, the length of the Order will usually be no more than three years, regardless of the age of the children. The principle will ensure that if the resulting equity for each party is considered sufficient to provide alternative accommodation, the Court will order house sales.

Custody of the children certainly does not mean the family home is there for the custodial parent. Section 28(A) of the Matrimonial Property Act 1976 requires that particular regard be given to the accommodation needs of the children. Section 28(A) is based on the need to provide a home for any minor dependent child of the marriage. In 1983 the Matrimonial Property Act was amended by the insertion of this Section, however, it does not detract from the perceived virtues of the 'clean break principle'. If the custodial parent fails to have an Occupation Order or cannot afford to buy the spouse's share in the home, the result is that the custodial parent and the children have to move out. It has been argued greater emphasis could be placed on giving non-earner custodial parents occupation of the home and there should be a presumption of that effect. It is quite clear when the custodial parent and the children finally leave the family home they suffer a drastic drop in their standard of living. The reality is, if there is not enough money for two households, it is difficult to apply the principle of Section 28(A).

Child Support

If the custodial parent goes on the Domestic Purposes Benefit, which is widely utilised, there is no legal obligation for the earner to assist the non-earner custodial parent directly. The custodial parent may apply for a Formula Assessment of the non-custodial parent's contribution to Child Support, pursuant to the Child Support Act 1991, if he or she goes on the Benefit. Under this Act the earner will be obliged to contribute to the State on the basis of a percentage of his or her net taxable income.

The custodial parent could make an urgent Application to Court and the Court could grant an urgent Maintenance Order whether or not the Child Support Agency has accepted the Child Support Application. The Application would only be granted if the Court considers the child to be in urgent need of financial assistance. Because of the ability to get emergency Benefit payments, this Section is hardly used at all by the Court (Section 116, Child Support Act 1991).

The earner pays to the State and is assessed for taxable net income of up to a $58,506.00 ceiling until 31 March 1996. If the earner's assessment is more than the DPB amount received, the custodial parent should receive the extra amount directly. However, in most cases, the earner pays the contribution to the State, the custodial parent receives the Domestic Purposes Benefit and there ends the matter. Before the Child Support Act came into play in 1991, the earner paid liable parent contributions and he or she may have also paid some extra money towards the non-earner to cover such expenses as school fees, orthodontic fees and music lessons. Now the earner may say he or she is not able to afford the extras because all the money goes to the State. The non-earner has no ability to get payment from the earner for the children outside the payment of the Domestic Purposes Benefit. There has been a suggestion in the recent Child Support Review that a greater proportion of the payment should be made to the custodial parent on a Benefit and not all to the State. If the earner cares for one or other children, the non-earner may also end up paying $10.00 payments to the earner from his or her Benefit. If the custodial parent decides not to apply for the DPB and support herself or himself and the children with Child Support payments, Family Support and perhaps working full-time, various difficulties will be encountered.

Although the fundamental intention of the Child Support Scheme is that parents have an obligation to support their children, whether they are living with them or not, the caregivers may experience the following difficulties:

1. Time delay

If the custodial parent applies for a Formula Assessment under the Child Support Act, he or she may experience a six week period before any payment will be received. There are many cases where custodial parents have waited for up to three months before seeing any money at all because of internal policies. The liable parent may be given options of how to pay the Child Support, such as payment by Direct Credit from a bank account. If the liable parent doesn't reply to the Inland Revenue Department within six weeks, he or she may be given another six weeks for a follow-up. The result of reluctant payers is that many custodial parents have no choice but to be on the DPB.

2. The earner resides overseas

There is no reciprocal arrangement for collection of Child Support in any overseas country. Even though Australia has a similar system, if the earner spouse disappears to Australia or another country, the custodial parent has no option but to go on the DPB or to rely on his or her own financial resources.

3. The earner is self employed

There is an ability of the self employed earner to hide income. Allowable deductions and losses reduce taxable income. The self-employed liable parent is permitted to seek at least 4 reassessments within one year. The liable parent must show at least 15 percent variation in income. He or she can choose an income year which may be a lean year to minimise child support. The non custodial parent may be hiding income via trusts and business devices. This all leads to less payment towards the children's care.

4. Ceiling

There is a net taxable income ceiling for earners. If the earner has a higher income than the ceiling, the children do not have the benefit of that income. The earner can earn as much as he or she wishes and only a percentage of the income will be taken into consideration. The ceiling, referred to previously in this paper, is $58,606.00.

5. The earner has arrears with the Child Support Agency

If the non-custodial parent goes into arrears, the collection of any money goes first to the oldest part of the debt, eg. penalties. The custodial parent can miss out completely if the non-custodial parent is always in arrears and it may be cheaper for that parent to do so.

6. Application for Suspension Order

When a liable parent applies for a Departure Order, an Ex Parte Application for Suspension may be filed with the application. These Orders suspend Child Support liability where a full hearing for a Departure is still pending. Some Judges immediately reduce the amount payable by the Liable Parent to $10.00 per week. The Suspension Order may immediately cut off a large portion of the caregiver's income, thus affecting the children's financial care.

7. Departure Orders

A Departure Application can be made to vary the Support Order upwards or downwards by either parent. Departure Orders are difficult to obtain. Since 1 July 1994, Review Officers have been appointed, rather than using the Family Court. However, the grounds for Departure Orders still have to be established.

8. Disentitlement to Legal Aid

A non-beneficiary caregiver's income may disentitle her or him to Legal Aid. It is expensive to apply for Orders through the Court. If the caregiver is a beneficiary and has any assets, such as a house, she or he may have to have a Charge registered over the house to Legal Services to pay back the legal fees.

9. Formula Assessment with new partner and children

If the non-custodial partner re-partners and has more children, the payments to the first family will be reduced. The formula is calculated on the payer's taxable income with a standard allowance for living costs. A living allowance for a person who re-partners and has four or more children living with them can mean he or she has a living allowance of approximately $27,208.00. This in turn reduces the amount payable as Child Support to the non-custodial parent's first family.

10. Matrimonial Property Act 1976 versus the Child Support Act 1991

Because the Child Support Act operates in isolation from the Matrimonial Property Act, there is no reason for parties to be interested in trade-offs of property in relation to future maintenance following separation.

Spousal Maintenance

Spousal maintenance should be regarded as an interim measure and is not widely sought after because it is difficult to get. The means that there will be no money in the household to assist the family other than the DPB or a basic contribution to Child Support.

Matrimonial Property

Custodial parents accepting less than 50 percent of the assets

Often the custodial parent will take less than a 50/50 split because of:

(a) Litigation

Litigation is expensive. Legal Aid is a loan not a grant.

(b) Violence

The custodial parent who has been subjected to physical and emotional abuse from their partners may continue to feel intimidated and frightened. They are sometimes forced to share their DPB with the non-custodial parent for access costs and they may prefer to settle for a lesser sum rather than face up to continuing legal costs.

(c) Children versus property

What has been referred to as 'custody blackmail' means the custodial parent may forgo part of the matrimonial property assets in exchange for custody which means that the children are financially worse off.

There is an ability to settle matrimonial property in favour of children. If the custodial parent would like to keep some of the property for the children, but cannot afford to buy a share of that property, he or she may consider Section 26 of the Matrimonial Property Act 1976. Such matrimonial property as a holiday house could be put in Trust with neither parent owning the property, but allowing their children to have the continued benefit of it.

There is no doubt that the custodial parent is financially disadvantaged on the break-up of the marriage. There are many perceived injustices of the law in the areas of Child Support, Spousal Maintenance and Matrimonial Property by both the liable parent and the custodial parent.

The current Minister of Justice has indicated that issues of matrimonial property legislation need to be re-addressed. There is no doubt there needs to be change in the legislation so that the children of a broken marriage are not caught in a poverty trap.

In a marriage break-up, the household income initially inevitably drops in both the earner's and non-earner's household. The children of these marriages should not be the financial victims.

The Legal Realities for Children and Families – Part Three: 'Reaching the Best Agreements for Children and Families'

Judge E O K Blaikie
District Court Judge with Family
and Youth Court Warrants, Dunedin

Introduction

This paper will deal with the following topics:

1. **Reaching Agreement – The Process**
   (a) Counselling
   (b) Mediation

2. **Welfare of Children**

3. **Roles of Participants in The Process**

This seminar examines many important issues affecting children and their parents when difficulties arise as a result of relationship problems, and subsequent changes during the periods of children's dependency on one or both of their parents. My comments will refer to the ways in which the Family Court deal with the problems arising from relationship difficulties experienced by parents and the methods employed in the court to reach a satisfactory resolution. It should be noted here that on a few occasions parental agreement concerning children may not, for a variety of reasons, be in the best interests of the children. In these situations the Court must regard the welfare of children as the paramount consideration which may result in the Court calling for independent and specialist evidence concerning the children, and subsequently imposing orders which do not accord with the wishes of the parents. This can be a complex issue.

The Family Court was established as a division of the District Court in 1981. Most of you will be aware that proceedings in the Family Court are private with an emphasis on informality. The Family Proceedings Act which governs the Court and the process deals with counselling judicial mediation with guidelines for the conduct of hearings in the court. Family Court Judges are warranted to preside in the courts and lawyers engaged in Family Court work have clear duties and obligations concerning information which they must provide their clients for the purposes of promoting either reconciliation or conciliation. This duty is also cast upon the Court and enables the Court to encourage or direct parties to attend counselling after proceedings have been filed and at any stage thereafter until final determination by way of Court decision.

The Court deals with wide ranging legal issues affecting children and their parents, such issues extending from the establishment of paternity of children through to ensuring that appropriate testamentary provision is made for dependants in the wills of adults. The court in New Zealand deals with numerous statutes enacted in New Zealand and is also bound by the provisions of the Hague Convention and the UN Convention on the rights of the child. Before departing this topic I refer to some recent legislative developments. One relates to the Bill which is currently before Parliament dealing with the substantial issue of domestic violence and a second matter concerns substantial changes proposed to the Adoption Legislation, in particular the suggested restrictions limiting step parent adoptions. Here the emphasis is on preservation of guardianship rights.

Before concluding these background comments I refer to the important issues and definitions of guardianship, custody and access. The Guardianship Act 1968 defines *guardianship* 'to include the right of control over the upbringing of a child, and includes all rights, powers and duties in respect of the person and upbringing of a child'. *Custody* means 'the right to possession and care of a child'. *Access* means 'access to a child by a parent who does not have custody of that child'. The Guardianship Act defines persons who are the legal guardians of children and enables parents and others to apply to the Court for an order appointing them guardians.

Reaching Agreement – The Process

The major components of this process are counselling and mediation.

(a) Counselling

Many commentators refer to the concept of the therapeutic intervention of the Family Court. Such a concept is in keeping with the philosophy of the Family Law Legislation and the duties imposed on counsel and the Court to explore ways in which conciliation can be achieved at all times. Usually the earliest intervention by the Court arises when one or two parents request counselling pursuant to Section 9 of the Family Proceedings Act. In that situation the Court is a facilitator for the counselling process to be arranged and undertaken, and it would be fair to say that those couples who request or are referred to counselling often do not require further assistance from the Court in the process which I am about to outline.

Most applications to the Court involving children, are governed by the Family Proceedings Act and the Guardianship Act. Many applications involving children made **immediately** following separation require an urgent response from the Court. Often two major issues emerge, the first being the difficult relationship between the parents and the second being need for the children's welfare to be addressed in regard to where they reside and the appropriate contact with each parent. It would be fair to say that the way in which the Court responds to and deals with these urgent applications can determine the attitude of the parties not just towards conciliation and attempts to reach agreement but towards the integrity of the Family Court itself. Further problems can arise when the Court makes interim orders on ex parte applications (without the knowledge of one parent) concerning children. Often the party against whom the order is made is aggrieved, not because of the necessity for the order but because the order was made in his or her absence. There are many examples in the courts throughout New Zealand where the fact that the first orders made were in the absence of one party, has effected that party's ability to engage in the Family Court process in a way in which the interests of the children are put first over and above the anger or personal needs of the adult. Occupation of the home is a further difficult issue for parents at the time when separation is contemplated by one or both parents, or has just taken place. This is a time when some parties come to the court feeling wounded or desperate for a variety of reasons. It is important to recognise the existence of, or potential for, these acute human emotions immediately following separation and that there is a distinct prospect that the welfare of the children will be affected by them. If agreements are to be negotiated at this stage it is important for the parties to understand that any agreements reached concerning the children immediately following separation should be on an interim basis and subject to a review at any time, either in the counselling process or before a Judge in the Family Court.

The concept of interim arrangements is also important for children themselves. It is likely that they, like their parents, will be in a state of bewilderment and uncertainty and it is imperative to ensure that the children do not feel or accept any responsibility for the problems experienced in the relationship of their parents. At this early stage it is useful in my view for the Court to make directions rather than impose orders. Although this may seem a matter of semantics there is a better prospect for agreement if parties are referred to counselling (in the stage immediately following separation) without Court imposed orders relating to the children.

There is however, one category of cases which requires a different approach by the Court, being cases involving domestic violence. At the present time the legislation enables the Court to make non-molestation, non-violence and occupation orders in favour of parents who are the victims of violence within a relationship. Those orders can and should be made as soon as possible if justified, and are usually made in the absence of the perpetrator of the violence. I have mentioned the Domestic Violence Bill. The Bill as enacted extends greatly the category of person who is entitled to apply for protection and it also imposes significant restrictions upon violent parents having unsupervised contact with children.

I now refer to the integrity of the Family Court and the desirability of engendering where possible, and appropriate, an atmosphere within the court which secures the trust of the participants. In this regard the counselling process plays a vital role in several ways. It must be recognised that the initial post separation period is often the time when the children are most at risk from the acute psychological pressure and abuse which can be extended by parents at a time of high emotion. I believe the counselling process in New Zealand with the extensive group of highly skilled and professionally trained counsellors is a significant component to the success of the Family Court. Without counselling in that post separation period couples often experience considerable difficulty in communicating and putting in place arrangements which are best for their children. Most Judges encounter cases on a regular basis where agreements cannot be reached concerning children because the parents have been unable to resolve the issues concerning their own relationship. The immediate example which surfaces in this category concerns a couple where one parent adamantly wishes the separation to continue whilst the other is anxious for a reconciliation. Within that scenario there are limitless possibilities of problems for not just the parents but more importantly the children. Resolution of the parental relationship (both accepting the separation) clears the path for agreements concerning the children. Professional counselling plays a vital role in achieving this resolution.

For my own part, I find it difficult to assist parties in reaching agreement concerning their children whilst there remain unresolved relationship problems. It is also important to recognise that resolution of relationship problems can take some considerable time, and again I return to the procedure whereby the Court, unless it is necessary for the protection or welfare of the children to make orders, can provide adequately for the children by imposing directions concerning residence and contact. It is also important for the Court to be alert to the benefits which parents can receive from counselling at any period of the dependency of the children. Counselling is a useful forum for parents to discuss arrangements agreed to or directed by the Court, and there will be in most cases further referrals to counselling when subsequent applications are made for custody, access or guardianship issues to be determined by the Court. Whilst the integrity of the Family Court process is important, it is equally important for there to be an integrity in the counselling process so that parties willingly return to that process for assistance. Counselling is an effective way of assisting parties to communicate more effectively. Development of good communication requires trust and respect, and I believe the skills of many counsellors assist in this regard. Many counselling reports refer to guardianship discussions. If counsellors can inform parents of their guardianship rights and responsibilities, this information often assists in the process of conciliation.

(b) Mediation

A mediation conference chaired by a Family Court Judge can be requested by either party, including their counsel or counsel for children, or can be directed by the Court at any stage of the proceedings. It is uncommon for a mediation conference to be convened before the counselling process has been attempted. The process of mediation in the Family Court of New Zealand is unique to some extent in that the conference is chaired by a Family Court Judge who has the power, not just to record agreements which have been reached between the parties, but to make orders with the consent of parties and preferably the consent of their counsel. The process of mediation has been available throughout the world for many years. New Zealand Family Court Judges receive training for mediation, and it has been interesting for us involved in the training to experience the views and approaches of overseas mediation experts. Mediation is described as being 'a cooperative model of dispute resolution. In its most pure form mediation is a process whereby two or more disputants engage the procedural direction of an independent mediator who leads the interview to find the issues, share information, general options and bargain. The mediator controls the process. The disputants retain control over the substance of the issues.' The sixth edition of Butterworths Family Law in New Zealand which is an extensive and particularly useful text on all Family Law issues, makes additional reference to mediation being 'mediation is goal orientated. It is designed to resolve specific issues within a short time-frame. It does not involve therapy'. Some of you will be aware of the process of mediation practised elsewhere in New Zealand and overseas. 'Pure' mediation practised overseas usually involves very extensive periods of time. The Family Court in New Zealand does not have resources for, nor are there expectations of, numerous and long mediations for parents seeking the assistance of the Court.

I have referred to the Family Law text published by Butterworths. Brooker and Friend Limited publish similar texts and both publish on a regular basis law reports of selected judgments delivered by Family Court Judges delivered throughout New Zealand. Most Family Courts have access to videos which parents are invited to view. These videos are invaluable in that they depict quite clearly the needs and welfare of children and the problems experienced by children whose parents are unable to communicate and cooperate.

The mediation conference is attended by parties, their lawyers at the party's request, and counsel appointed to represent children. On occasions support persons for either party can, with the approval of the Judge, be invited to attend. Current partners or spouses of the parties and extended families are included in this category.

Earlier I mentioned the need for Judges to recognise the situation parents have reached in regard to their own relationship. In mediation it is also important for Judges to be aware of other fundamental issues. I refer in particular to questions of safety for one or more of the participants; the use of the mediation process by one of the parents to continue exerting power and control over the other parent; the need for the mediator to ensure that the parties have in the process the confidence to express clearly their own views; the awareness of the mediator of power and control issues and a clear explanation at the commencement of the conference of rules of conduct and consequences to the parties if agreements can be negotiated.

The New Zealand Family Court mediation process has some clear advantages. The mediator, by virtue of his or her position as a Family Court Judge is perceived by the parties as being a person with authority. A Judge is in a position to provide realistic testing of parents' proposals. This technique can often help parents in moving towards agreement, particularly in cases where proposals are unlikely to be supported or endorsed if the matter came before a Judge at a formal hearing. The ability of the mediator to make court orders with the consent of both parties can provide parents with security and peace of mind and has the substantial advantage of reduction of financial costs which otherwise would be incurred at a formal hearing. To conclude this topic I also mention that the mediation process is one which can dilute personal and long term damage to parents which would otherwise arise at a court hearing involving cross examination and associated tension and distrust.

Often the mediation conference is the first occasion when parents actually attend the court. Accordingly the comments I made earlier regarding the integrity of the Family Court and the desirability of parents having confidence in the Family Court are equally applicable to the parties attending their first mediation conference. The mediation conference can develop in several ways. Often parties are referred back to counselling, either by agreement or by direction of the Court, as a result of issues raised at the conference itself. The conference may also discuss procedural aspects relating to the appointment of counsel to represent the children or for the appointment of a report writer pursuant to section 29A of the Guardianship Act who would provide a specialist report on some specific issues relating to the children. On occasions mediation conferences are adjourned for a further conference when interim arrangements are agreed upon with the express request that those arrangements be reviewed within a time frame at a later conference.

In many respects the way in which a mediation conference is conducted depends upon the personal preferences and skills of the particular Judge. Some conferences proceed smoothly with agreements being reached and recorded as consent Court orders. Other conferences because of the personality of the parties have the potential for generating further personal abuse and threats, and on those occasions a Judge would terminate the conference without further discussion and probably make directions for the matter to be set down for hearing. On many occasions reasonable discussions ensure at the conference which may not result in any agreements at all. In those situations the conference can be a useful process in that the parties can at a later stage reflect on the issues raised at the conference and the discussions which then took place. Often we experience situations where formal agreements are presented to the Court in the weeks following the mediation conference which would indicate that the process has assisted the parties in concluding arrangements for their children. In these cases the conference has presented a framework for resolution after appropriate reflection by the parents.

I now propose to comment on the structure of the mediation conference itself. I will also refer to various techniques which I find useful in providing assistance to the parents in reaching appropriate agreements for their children. In this regard I refer to the first mediation conference attended by the parties after counselling has been undertaken and before either counsel for the children is appointed and a consideration given for Social Welfare or specialist reports. At this conference I encourage the parties to consider guardianship and communication issues. I intend now to deal with each issue in further detail.

Guardianship Issues

Often parties come to the court without a clear understanding of guardianship rights and responsibilities. A discussion assisted by the Judge on guardianship matters often produces positive results and outcomes. An understanding of guardianship rights and responsibilities can be advantageous to the conference process in that it can achieve one or more of the following:

1. An acceptance by both parents that each has an equal responsibility for and each has separate rights in regard to major decisions relating to the children.

2. Setting an agenda for discussion on non threatening topics such as the schooling and health needs of the children.

3. A balancing of power whereby the participation of the non custodial parent can be encouraged in decision making.

4. An opportunity for the parties to focus on the needs of the children rather than their own particular wishes.

On many occasions the discussion on guardianship issues can lead parties towards agreement on custodial and access arrangements. This can occur as a direct result of the communication which occurs on the guardianship topics and the development of trust which can emerge during that discussion. It is quite common for a parent without custody of children to commence the conference in an angry and belligerent frame of mind, exhibiting signs of frustration and limited trust towards the other. I believe the issue of guardianship is a powerful topic and one if discussed appropriately can aid the manner in which the mediation conference progresses.

Communication

This issue, along with guardianship understandings, is one of the major components, not just to a successful mediation but to the parents ability to make proper arrangements for the children on a regular basis.

Many of you may consider the issue of communication to be a self evident and require no further comment. Again I am referring to my personal preferences and often I will commence the conference by enquiring of the parties as to whether they are speaking to each other. That question invariably produces a plethora of responses. Often I will use a technique by asking the parties to recall, if they are able to, the last occasion when communication for each parent was satisfactory to them, and to discuss why the situation was acceptable at that time and what changes have occurred since. This issue of communication is present at all times and if the courts can assist parents with their communication then that is a major step towards proper arrangements being made for the children. On occasions parties have to be encouraged to restrict communication to written messages until they are able to develop skills sufficient to avoid constant verbal altercations over the children. Furthermore it is important to explain to parents that effective and regular communication between parents which is observed by children and is about the children can provide reassurance for the children in many respects.

A further technique which I use in an effort to help the parties with their communication difficulties involves requesting each parent to talk about their children at the mediation conference. By asking the parents to describe their children's personalities, school progress, health situation, particular interests and diet arrangements can be a useful tool for promoting discussion on non threatening topics. Often parents, to their individual surprise, are in agreement when they describe the particular needs and development stages of their children.

A mediator can often observe dramatic changes in parents during the discussion on guardianship and communication topics. Personally I like to remind and record with the parents the positive changes which I observe in their attitudes towards each other, their body language, their listening capabilities, their reactions and indeed the tone of their voice. By introducing and reinforcing the positive changes which occur during the mediation the opportunity can then arise to contrast the negatives portrayed by each parent which are usually much more apparent at the commencement of the discussions. To finalise the topic of communication I believe mediators in the Family Court have a responsibility to ensure that correct terminology is used. For example reference by one parent to my children should be discouraged, the parties could be encouraged to refer to contact with the children rather than custody or access, the parties should refrain from referring to the other as he or she and instead use names and constant reminders should be given to the parties to focus on their children's needs rather than their personal desires.

I now propose to list various techniques which I use and the goals and aspirations which I have when parties attend for mediation. Clearly the list is not exhaustive and all mediators have preferences to suit their particular styles and personalities. Some of the techniques referred to are skills which counsellors have been using for a long time and are accepted as being appropriate for dispute resolution. The examples are:

1. Diverting extensive discussion by the parties on historical issues.

2. Insisting at the outset on clear rules for the mediation discussion.

3. Requesting one parent to acknowledge and state the parenting strengths and ability of the other parent, and if such acknowledgement is made enquiring from that parent as to when the acknowledgement was last made to the other parent.

4. Encouraging parents to discuss and focus on consistent rules in each house for the children. Bedtimes, television programmes, suitable children activities and diet arrangements come within this category.

5. Guiding parents to discuss precise and actual arrangements for their children. For example which parent is to be responsible for transporting the children from one house to the other, and at what time and where the children will be when collected from or returned to either parent.

6. Ensuring that the mediator, and indeed the other parent, understanding what one parent is saying. The techniques involving reflecting and repetition are useful in this category.

7. Recognising and applauding the parties for effective communication during the conference.

8. Introducing appropriate humour.

9. Reassuring the parents that any agreements or orders made at the conference can be varied by further agreement between the parties or by subsequent court order. In this regard it is important to stress to parties that arrangements made now for children may not be appropriate for a particular child because of his or her changing needs, personalities and wishes.

On many occasions mediation conferences are conducted involving parties who have been unable to communicate effectively throughout their relationship and the task for achieving any improvement in this regard is major to say the least. In an ideal world all parents should communicate effectively regarding arrangements for their children. Question does arise however as to the amount of assistance and Family Court resources which could or should be made available for parents who blatantly refuse to accept responsibility for the problems they cause for their children and who return to the court on a regular basis because of their inability to resolve issues themselves. In my view one of the underlying goals should be for parents to understand that ultimately they have to accept personal responsibility and this responsibility extends to their behaviour as parents and guardians of children and must encompass a basic level of communication to achieve appropriate contact between parents and both children.

To conclude this topic I wish to refer briefly to the times scheduled for mediation conferences and the allocation of time for mediation conferences on a regular basis in the Family Court. Conferences are scheduled for one hour and usually this time is not exceeded unless progress in the conference is sufficient for the time to be extended. Often Judges will adjourn a conference briefly to enable parents to confer with their legal counsel, and on most occasions they will return with agreements which can be recorded or consents for orders to be made. Difficulties can arise in some courts where pre scheduled mediation time is not provided causing substantial delays in conferences being convened before a Judge. Some courts schedule each week parts of the week for mediation conferences and this enables some conferences to be reconvened at short notice and this I believe is in accordance with the philosophy of the Family Law Legislation and the responsibilities most of us have towards conciliation. Personally I am very supportive of the mediation process and I am quite convinced that any agreements reached between parents in counselling or mediation are more likely to be in the best interests of the children, adhered to and respected by the adults and less likely to produce continuing bitter and acrimonious litigation.

The Welfare of Children

This is the issue which all Judges must consider as being the first and paramount consideration in all cases involving children in the Family Court. The Guardianship Act 1968 (section 23) records 'the Court shall regard the welfare of the child as the first and paramount consideration. The Court shall have regard to the conduct of any parent to the extent only that such conduct is relevant to the welfare of the child.' In reaching conclusions relating to the welfare of children Judges usually have to weigh up and balance many and numerous factors. I am sure that counsellors are aware of and familiar with this fundamental principle. Report writers are requested to provide information to the Court to assist the Court in reaching conclusions and making decisions which best serve the needs of and meet the welfare of children. Trained Family Court lawyers will be aware of the many factors which impact on the needs and welfare of children. This knowledge should assist lawyers in carrying out their duties and obligations concerning conciliation. Most parents claim that they are 'doing what is best for the children'. The numerous reported and unreported decisions of Family Court Judges, High Court Judges, Court of Appeal Judges and Judges from jurisdictions overseas provide, in many cases, invaluable assistance to individual Judges required to determine a guardianship, custody or access dispute. In this paper I propose to comment on some factors, not all, which regularly occur in most cases where parents seek the assistance of the Family Court through counselling, mediation, and if agreement is not reached a court hearing. The factors are:

(a) Parenting Ability

This issue required little explanation and usually represents a viewpoint of support or criticism by both parents. As custody involves the day to day care of a child, the comparative parenting abilities of each parent is always a relevant factor.

(b) Attachment

This issue has caused considerable discussion amongst professionals and often attracts the definition of bonding. In cases involving infant and very young children the degree of attachment to the respective parents is usually quite clear. The Guardianship Act 1968 specifically precludes a presumption in favour of one parent because of the gender of that parent, thereby removing the earlier 'mother principle' for young children, so the issue of attachment is but one factor if the Court is requested to comment on or exercise its discretion in determining the welfare of a child.

(c) Immediate compared with long-term arrangements

Early in this paper I referred to the many difficulties encountered by parents immediately following separation. That is a crucial time for children and it is imperative for their basic needs to be met including their accommodation, continuation of schooling and reassurances to the effect that they will continue to have contact with both parents.

(d) Children's wishes

This can be a complex issue. Often children express wishes and preferences to please a particular parent whom they perceive to be upset because of the separation. In other situations the children will often express a preference to reside with one parent who expresses antagonistic and negative views regarding the other parent. In that situation the child is frightened of the parent's reaction to their expression of preference in favour of the other parent. In cases involving older children the Court has a responsibility to ascertain their wishes. Those wishes can be taken into account to such an extent having regard to the age and maturity of the child. Younger children should not be asked to express a preference and to do so could constitute a form of abuse of the child.

(e) Children remaining together

As a general rule the courts will encourage parents to make arrangements so that children reside together. Research indicates that siblings, particularly immediately following the separation of their parents, look to each other for support and reassurance. A separation often has a traumatic effect on children and to separate them could add to the considerable level of stress which they are experiencing.

(f) Parental understanding of health and education needs

Most parents have aspirations for their children's education. Some parents are better equipped than others to ensure regular attendance of children at school, to assist with homework, to become involved with school activities and to make regular contact with teachers for interviews and school meetings. Regrettably children can experience health problems as a direct result of the family stresses which occur following separation. The onset of asthma or bed wetting are common occurrences. Accordingly an understanding of health and education needs of children, and an ability to meet those needs, are factors which guide the Court in determining the way in which the children's welfare will be met.

(g) The attitude of parents toward each other

The following examples illustrate the destructive effect on children which can occur through the inappropriate attitude of one parent. I refer to, the parent who wishes to continue punishing the other parent, the parent who remains so distraught and angry that he or she is unable to focus on the needs of the child, the parent who is motivated by financial obligations, the parent who seeks custody to replace the loss of the other parent, and the parent who is unwilling to cooperate to ensure that adequate and proper contact occurs between the children and the other parent.

(h) The availability of each parent

Often some parents are quite unrealistic in their proposals for the care of children, having regard to their employment commitments. It is also comment for some parents to indicate their intention to terminate their employment in their quest for a custody order in their favour. In those circumstances it is usual for the Court to encourage extreme caution.

The above issues and associated examples are some of the matters which counsel for children must address and advocate on behalf of their clients. To conclude this topic I refer to the following concise statement provided by Professor Wade to the recent Family Law Conference in Wellington. In my view these statements deserve wide and extensive distribution and publication. I am sure all the children would be reassured to know that their parents have very clear principles as outlined.

A Child's Rights

- A CHILD has the right to love each parent without being subject to the other partner's hurt or anger.
- A CHILD has the right to develop and independent and meaningful relationship with each parent and to enjoy the uniqueness of each parent and each home.
- A CHILD has the right to extended family relationships which include grandparents, aunts, uncles, cousins, and others and to appreciate the unique differences of each side of his or her family and not have these differences referred to as 'better' or 'worse'.
- A CHILD has the right to be free from questions about the other parent's private life.
- A CHILD has the right to see his or her parents treat each other in a courteous and respectful manner.
- A CHILD has the right to develop and maintain activities and friends without fear of losing time with a parent.
- A CHILD has the right to be a CHILD without having to assume adult and/or parental roles or duties.

A Parent's Rights

- A PARENT has the right to love and nurture one's child without harassment from the other parent.
- A PARENT has the right to receive respect and courtesy and the obligation to show respect and courtesy.
- A PARENT has the right to attend and participate in a child's special activities.
- A PARENT has the right to information regarding a child's physical, mental and emotional health.
- A PARENT has the right during parenting time to follow one's own standards, beliefs and style of child-rearing without interference from the other parent.
- A PARENT has the right to a separate and private life.

Roles of Participants

This section provides a brief summary of the roles of various people who provide assistance to parties, children and the Court during the process.

(a) Family Court Coordinator

This person has a key role in, firstly, ensuring that appropriate and prompt counselling is arranged, and secondly in engaging report writers and arranging appointments of counsel for children.

(b) Court Staff

Effective staff members in the Family Court should understand not just their clerical duties and responsibilities but also some of the stresses experienced by parents following separation. An ability to listen and demonstrate sensitivity is a commendable quality for court staff.

(c) Counsellors

Their responsibilities have been described at some length earlier in this paper. They, like Judges, are from time to time required to engender an atmosphere of trust for the parties. This has particular relevance to cases where one party is unwilling to attend counselling in the presence of the other. In many cases the fears of the unwilling party can be dispelled by firm skilful and professional counsellors.

(d) Counsel for Parties

Experienced Family Court counsel will not only carry out their obligations concerning conciliation on the part of their clients, but will explain to parties all options which should be considered when considering best arrangements for children. Some counsels through limited experience in the Family Court, or by promoting an adversarial approach, can have a considerable impact on the attitude of their clients. This often leads to the preparation and filing of acrimonious affidavits containing irrelevant detail and damaging allegations. The role of counsel at the mediation conference is one of support rather than actors intervention on behalf of their clients. Reports from the Children and Young Persons Service can be invaluable. The role of a social worker is however much more extensive. I refer in particular to families where care and protection issues arise, and the obligations on the Director-General through the Children and Young Persons Service to ensure that children are protected, safe from abuse, and have proper and appropriate supports put in place for their welfare. Whilst it is desirable to secure the agreement of parents when care and protection issues arise social workers have an overriding responsibility if agreement cannot be reached between parents to seek appropriate orders in the Family Court which meet the particular needs of the children concerned.

(e) Specialist Report Writers

The information which these trained specialists can provide can in some cases determine the outcome for children. Again the Family Court in New Zealand is fortunate in having a group of trained professionals who possess the skills to obtain appropriate information and report appropriately to the Court. Often the reports which are usually made available to parties and their counsel in providing independent assessment can assist parties in reaching agreements concerning custody and access issues. A recent practice note issued by the Principle Family Court Judge provides clear guidelines concerning the responsibility of specialist report writers and should assist them in the quite difficult tasks requested of them by the Court. I am aware of the differing views concerning the appropriate terminology used by report writers which could be construed as expressing either conclusions, opinions or indeed recommendations. On the one hand an expression of recommendations can be perceived as an attempt by the report writer to usurp the responsibility of the Judge in determining the issues. On the other hand some report writers consider the issues to be clearly established as a result of their enquiries and feel that the reference to recommendations can result in the parties being guided towards agreement. I believe reference to conclusions or summary following an extensive and balance report can provide appropriate indications to parents concerning the report writer's views which might not be determinative of the final decision to be reached which is the responsibility of the Court.

(f) Education and Health Professionals

The information which these people can provide to the Court is often crucial to the parties and the Court during the process. Many people in the education field have reported on the behaviour and attitude of children at school being indicative of the stress and lack of security at home. The school classroom is on many occasions the venue for children to speak positively regarding access visits or to express apprehension and fears concerning contact with a particular parent. Often the school environment is the only safe haven for children where they receive appropriate care and attention and encouragement in their particular pursuits. Likewise health professionals are requested from time to time to provide information to parents and the Court concerning health needs of children. Often one parent complains about the lack of information provided to that parent by the other concerning the health and education of the children. This is a guardianship issue referred to earlier. The problem can be compounded when teachers, doctors and other professionals elect to withhold information when requested by a parent and it is therefore important for the professionals to understand their obligations in this regard. Refusing to divulge information to a parent can increase the level of frustration and thwart the efforts of many to assist parties in cooperative communication. The Court will usually encourage both parents to attend school meetings, teacher interviews and appointments with medical professionals. To conclude this topic I refer to the opportunities available for active participation by both parents in children's pre-school activities. Research would indicate that involvement by both parents at playgroup, kindergarten and related pre-school institutions provide considerable benefit to children. The benefits however dissipate rapidly when parents use these opportunities for manipulation purposes or to continue their ongoing arguments and lack of cooperation.

(g) Care & Protection Coordinator

Care and protection coordinators have a statutory function as prescribed in the Children, Young Persons and Their Families Act. I have made reference to the coordinators because their task is in some respects similar to a Presiding Judge at a mediation conference. The family group conference forms a crucial part of the care and protection legislation in New Zealand. A professionally conducted family group conference involving parents, social workers, extended family, professionals and counsel can achieve similar outcomes to those achieved at a mediation conference whereby children are protected, their welfare is enhanced, and their needs met. Successful coordinators possess the personal skills and attributes which can dissipate distrust on the part of parents towards the Children's and Young Persons Service and encourage parents to address the needs of their children.

(h) Support Groups

The presence of support groups, particularly for women in destructive or violent relationships should be welcomed by the Court. Provided the presence of the support groups do not impinge on issues of power and control parties should be aware that they can request in appropriate circumstances the presence of support personnel in the courtroom during the mediation or hearing process.

(i) Partners or Spouses of Parties

Their presence at mediation will normally depend on the circumstances of the case and the attitude and preference of the Presiding Judge. It should be acknowledged however that on occasions the presence of the other parent's partner or new spouse can cause considerable anxiety or anger for the other parent. On other occasions it is entirely appropriate for such persons to be present for part of a mediation conference where particular issues are being discussed which may involve diet and health requirements for children whilst visiting the other parent or for arranging appropriate channels of communication. On many occasions the new partners of parents can play a major and positive role in reducing levels of anger and encouragement of good communication between the respective parents.

(j) Counsel for Children

This is a crucial role requiring special training and advocacy skills. Effective counsel for children will ensure that all relevant information is before the Court, evidence is appropriately tested, parents are informed of the issues and children are protected from unnecessary interviewing and observation. On many occasions counsel for children can provide considerable assistance to parties in encouraging agreement which will secure the best arrangements for the children. On some occasions they need to possess the appropriate skills where by the interests of the children can be advanced which may in some circumstances be in conflict with the children's express wishes. Effective counsel for children should possess an ability to relate to children, have an understanding of child development issues and be able to explain to children factual matters having regard to appropriate understanding levels and time frames which can be understood and grasped by young people. Counsel for children will usually work in close liaison with the family court coordinator and whilst their tasks and responsibilities are independent of each other their combined roles usually provide effective case management in ensuring that resolution is achieved without unnecessary delay and in an appropriate manner.

Summary

This paper has attempted to address some of the relevant issues which are confronted by various people working in or for the Family Court. I have not referred in particular detail to the matters which arise for consideration at a defended hearing. At that stage in the process the parties are seeking adjudication rather than conciliation through counselling and mediation. The hearing process is also applicable for the small number of cases where counselling and mediation is inappropriate. That state of affairs can arise through a variety of reasons but usually because of personality problems of one or both parents to such a degree that the prospect of the parties reaching appropriate agreements and adhering to those agreements are minimal. There are other cases where despite the best efforts of parties and all concerned agreement cannot be reached and the Court is accordingly required to determine the issues on the available evidence. Assisting parties in reaching agreements through counselling or mediation can be a difficult but rewarding task. This requires a level of skill and a commitment from all participants in the various roles each plays. This is one of the reasons why the Family Law in New Zealand is described as involving teamwork and cooperation. Presumably if the same level of cooperation could be achieved between parents, as exhibited by the professionals engaged in the Family Court, then the welfare of children in New Zealand would be well and truly enhanced.

To conclude – in many cases one of the most persuasive factors in helping parents reach agreement is *time*.

Summing Up and Close for the Day

Judge Patrick D Mahony
Principal Family Court Judge

As we take time to draw together the day's themes, it is noteworthy that this first seminar of the Children's Issues Centre has attracted wide interest with participants from around New Zealand representing a significant range of disciplines.

The first paper by Professor Pool on family demographic changes left me with the need to study further the depth and range of content of materials which he put before us.

His paper brought home the importance of accurate information as a basis for policy making and legislation without which there is a very real danger that important social policy will be based on myth. He also stressed the importance of making proper distinctions, for example, the distinction between 'household' and 'family' in understanding statistical information. This distinction places in perspective the rather disturbing figures for Maori solo parents. Linked with that issue is the need for the skilled interpretation of statistics in drawing broad conclusions and formulating social policy.

Professor Pool's paper laid the foundation for the presentations which followed and indeed for the whole seminar. The need for networking and interdisciplinary exchange became more apparent as the day progressed. Finally, the Professor gave a message of optimism justified by a comparison between the young people of today with those whom he described as 'the baby boomers'. It is so very easy in this whole field of family change, often described as family breakdown, to develop a negative mind set and an air of pessimism.

Professor Smith's overview of research on the effect of separation on children provides a particularly useful analysis for those involved in clinical practice and individual cases, including Judges and lawyers, who do not have the time and may not have the skills to understand the close analysis of individual research projects. For myself, the general conclusions referred to by Professor Smith as a result of her comparative study, reflect my experience in the Family Court.

Her paper emphasises the needs of children arising out of the time it takes some children to get over the separation of their parents, and the impact of severe parental conflict on children. Her call for qualitative research is of particular importance. Most of the research in this area has been quantitative. It is now time to turn our attention to the ways in which the negative aspects of separation and divorce can be contained for children and the most made of it as a time for healing. The ecology of separation, central to Professor Smith's theme, provides a framework within which this issue can be considered. Her paper again drew attention to the importance of the social sciences in formulating and applying policy affecting families.

Professor Hopa's presentation referred to the impact of social changes on whanau in a rather unique way given her intimate knowledge from her position within Maoridom and her professional experience. She referred to the effect of urbanisation; Maori women's control of their fertility; changing values within Maori families; the sharp decline in Maori fertility; the changing role of Kaumatua and Quia; the three generation families; the changing dynamics and emerging patterns within whanau. She elaborated in a practical way on Professor Pool's distinction between household and family and the impact on households of extended family and Maori hospitality. She referred to the impact of ghettos and the effect of employment policy. It is of interest to note the way in which the Children, Young Persons and Their Families Act sets out the principles for the care and protection of children in the context of family, rather than in relation to parents. Without attempting definition, the Act refers to whanau, hapu and iwi and sets out extensive policies and principles developed following wide consultation with Maori by the Select Committee.

Professor Hopa ended on a note of optimism. She said that Maori will survive because they are a resilient, adaptable people. She referred to the Iwi Development Plan aimed at restoring a sense of peoplehood and control over resources.

The next session, involving a number of adults and a young person speaking about the effects of separation and family re-grouping, brought us again to the realisation that in this area we are dealing with the lives and welfare of people. We were brought face to face with the honesty and courage of individuals speaking about private aspects of their lives to this group of strangers, to assist in our understanding from a personal perspective of problems which we often have to look at on a broader scale.

The presentation by a university lecturer who described himself as almost pathologically unable to be ruffled, yet reaching his flash point in anger and the difficulties in self control which that entailed, brings home the extent and range of human temperament and conduct which will have to be considered under the new Domestic Violence legislation when issues of violence within families and future contact with children have to be considered.

'Sarah's' story exemplified some of the conclusions drawn to our attention by Professor Smith referring to the years which it sometimes takes for children to readjust following separation and the need for honesty in dealing with children during what is also a critical period for them. She also demonstrated the resilience of young people to emerge from years of parental conflict, especially where some help and support are available to them.

The presentation by Mark Henaghan demonstrated the growing focus on children and their rights and interests in the process of family break-up. He highlighted the role of family law and the interface with social sciences, in deciding on outcomes for children. The fact that the '**welfare of the child**', which is the critical issue in this whole area, is not defined, but is a matter for judgement by the Court again points to the need for Judges to have access to the best research available with respect to all of the issues impacting on the welfare of children in the social and family context in which they have to grow up.

His paper also demonstrated the need for the law to adapt to changing times, values and needs. In this context, he referred to developments in the law in both England and Australia where notions of custody and access have been replaced by new labels of Parental Responsibility, Residence Orders and Contact Orders.

He also referred to the International Convention on the Rights of the Child, emphasising a shift from welfare issues to rights issues in dealing with children, and the way in which international law in this area is influencing and creating consistency of approach from one country to another. Through this movement, what is happening in other jurisdictions is relevant for those who have to formulate and apply the law here. The Family Courts of New Zealand and Australia are closely linked and both have strong links with the Courts in North America and more recently in England.

Annis Somerville referred to matrimonial property, child support and spousal maintenance. These are areas where the law has not adjusted well to changing social needs and where more reliance on information which could be provided by social scientists may have led to more equitable arrangements.

When the Matrimonial Property Act of 1976 was passed, it created a new and innovative regime for division of property based on the premise that marriage was a partnership of equals. In applying that policy at the end of the marriage however, it fails to recognise that some obligations assumed as part of the marriage contract are ongoing. The clean break principle does not serve well the parent who shoulders the main responsibility for continuing the parenting role for the children of the marriage. The equal division of property often leaves such a parent in a very unequal position in relation to the other partner, who is free to pursue a career, often with a high level of income.

Provisions with respect to spousal maintenance, which also incorporate the clean break principle, fail those wives who, as part of their marriage arrangements, put their energies into the marriage and family, thereby depriving themselves of the opportunity to pursue a work related career. It is inequitable that in their middle years, such women may be reduced to penury, at a time when their income-earning opportunities are reduced to a minimum, because of the strong presumption that each party be self-supporting from the time a marriage is dissolved.

Judge Blaikie's paper explained the Family Court process with emphasis on opportunities for conciliation and the role of the Judge in particular in mediation with the parties. He stressed the way in which the Family Court is able to facilitate settlements with the parties retaining control as to how their own disputes are managed and brought to a conclusion in a way which meets their particular family circumstances.

May I summarise by itemising the following conclusions which I think emerge from today's sessions:

1. Both the morning and afternoon papers and the session on individual personal experiences have laid a foundation for the extensive discussion allowed for in tomorrow's programme and provide a structure for the panel in general discussions to which most of the time will be devoted.

2. There is a vital need for communication across disciplines in order to develop approaches and outcomes which in an holistic way meet the needs of families and family members going through change.

3. Policy and law must be based on good scientific information, that is, sound and relevant research provided by the social sciences.

4. The social sciences are also vital in guiding clinicians, social workers, counsellors, judges and lawyers in developing what may be called 'best practice' for resolving family issues.

5. The partnership which already exists between the universities and academics on the one hand, and the practising professions and those working with the Courts on the other, needs to be recognised and consciously fostered.

6. There is room for a sense of optimism to be developed in this whole area of families in transition. This emerges from the papers of Professors Pool and Hopa and in the timely call for qualitative research from Professor Smith.

7. Although most people here are involved in areas of practice with families and children, they have been attracted in significant numbers to a seminar in which the first paper was presented by a demographer, followed by other papers dealing with sociological issues. There is, I believe, a clear message here for the Centre, of the appetite which we who work on a day-to-day basis with families have for better information and understanding of the underlying issues as a sound basis for improving the quality and effectiveness of our work.

Trying to Understand and Interpret the Child's Perspective

Max Gold
Department of Education, University of Otago

When parents separate and divorce, custody and access of children are sometimes a matter of dispute. To assist parents to resolve these disputes, the Family Court provides a process of counselling, mediation with a Judge, and finally a Court Hearing to determine the matter. This process recognises that, when children's welfare is at stake, decisions have to be made to give the parties some certainty about their future living circumstances.

Many parents agree upon issues such as custody and access of children with minimal assistance from the Court. Locally, somewhere around 80 percent of parents who separate, reach agreement before engaging in the process, or with the assistance of counselling. It is the remaining 20 percent of family situations which are the most problematic and difficult to resolve, which I wish to discuss today.

Professionals such as Psychiatrists, Psychologists and Psychotherapists are sometimes engaged by the Family Court to evaluate family situations, and provide opinions to the Court on a range of issues. Issues which frequently arise include, the attachment of the children to each parent, the strengths and challenges each parent faces in parenting their children, the children's opinion regarding custody and access, and the future situation which might best advance the interests of the children involved. Training which professionals such as Psychologists receive in child development, communication and family dynamics and their experience of working with children and families, provides them with a framework to evaluate family situations. For professionals to be able to understand the point of view of the children involved in family breakups, it is necessary to look at the whole family picture.

As a Psychologist working in the Family Court over the past ten years, I have found a framework which involves applying qualitative evaluation methodology (Patton 1987, Guba and Lincoln 1981) to be very useful. It is this framework which I now wish to discuss. Please note that I am asserting that qualitative evaluation methodology provides a framework to evaluating situations involving complex interactions between people. I am not saying that it is the framework which all professionals should use.

Qualitative evaluation methodology provides a means of evaluating the complex, intricate and somewhat 'messy' interactions between people in natural settings (Guba and Lincoln 1981). It provides information about situations which is credible – that is, believable to the participants, and auditable – that is, a fellow professional, looking at the same information available to the first professional, should be able to see the sense in the conclusions reached. Three sets of data are important in any qualitative evaluation.

Firstly **direct observations** of family members interacting in their usual living circumstances are a highly important source of information. People usually relax more in their home setting. An astute observer is likely to gain important information about family relationships , particularly those between parents and children, from being present to observe these in home settings.

Secondly, **indepth interviews** with family members and other important people such as the children's teachers, can provide a rich source of experience and perspectives with which to view issues involving the children. These interviews often 'flesh out' the picture one is able to obtain from direct observations, in that people interviewed can comment from a history of interacting with family members.

Thirdly, **analysing records** the family may have kept of their life together may also add to information from observations and interviews. Records such as diaries, photograph albums and children's Plunket Books may provide additional information supporting claims made by either parent about the role they have played in parenting their children.

The credibility of information arising from a qualitative evaluation is enhanced by the variety of methods which have been used to collect it. That is, information about each of the issues to be addressed comes from combining data gathered from direct observations, interviews and analysis of records. Credibilty of information gathered is also established by having family members view and comment on information arising from observations and interviews.

The information collected during a qualitative evaluation is combined to provide a basis upon which to offer an opinion on each of the issues to be addressed by the Report Writer. Each of the parties involved in the dispute may not necessarily agree with the opinion offered. However they should clearly see the rationale upon which the opinion is based. It is my view that the opinion is likely to be more readily accepted by the parties, if it is based upon credible information provided from a competent qualitative evaluation process.

There are many reasons why it is desirable to follow a thorough qualitative evaluation process, such as that outlined above, when trying to understand a child's perspective of their family.

When parents are in dispute over issues such as custody and access, they often have a vested interest in presenting a selective perception of their involvement with the children. There is sometimes a tendency to distort, or delete from their partner's contribution to parenting, and to generalise about their own efforts. There is also a tendency for parents to confuse their own needs, with the needs of the child. It is not until all parties have been interviewed, observations conducted and records analysed, that a more complete picture emerges, in which hopefully all pieces of the family 'jigsaw' fit together.

Similarly children may initially present a point of view which does not accurately represent the situation which would serve their interests long-term. Children's opinions can be influenced by those of important other people like parents. Children may echo sentiments expressed by their mother or father. Their opinion may be swayed by advantages parents have pointed out to them regarding one situation versus the other. Children's opinion can also be 'bought' with money, toys, sweets, or more frequent access to enjoyable experiences, such as trips to McDonalds. Children's opinions can also be swayed by preceding events. If they have recently experienced a disagreement with either parent, then they are more likely to express a detrimental point of view about that parent. Generally, the younger children are, the more likely it is that their opinion is susceptible to being influenced. Influences on a child's opinion are likely to become apparent during an intensive qualitative evaluation of the family situation.

There are many advantages then, in employing a qualitative evaluation process to try to understand a child's point of view in custody and access disputes in the Family Court.

The next issue I wish to consider, is the use which is made of the opinion expressed by the child, in Family Court matters. Frequently the child's viewpoint is not accessed in custody and access disputes between parents. There are good reasons for not involving the children. When parents are in conflict, children can experience conflicting loyalties to each parent. They may feel they are being placed in a situation where they have to choose between two loving parents. This can be very distressing for children. However, it is also stressful for children to feel that they are being left out of the decision-making process or, that their opinion is not being taken into account. Professionals in the Family Court often attempt to mini-mise the detrimental effects of the process on children by focussing soley on the adults in the decision-making process. If children's opinion is accessed, this often happens prior to the concluding third-stage of the process, when a Counsel for the Child is appointed or a Specialist Report is obtained, prior to a Hearing. My con-tention is, that there is a case for obtaining the opinion of school-aged children regarding custody and access, in a child-friendly way, at a much earlier stage in the Family Court process. I believe that if a professional were employed by the Court to interview children prior to parents entering into Mediation with a Judge, children would feel recognised and included in the process, and their opinion may be influential in resolving some of the more contentious cases during Mediation.

Next, I wish to discuss an issue which has been at the forefront of my mind for some time when I am considering the effects of separation and divorce on children. As a Psychologist I am often accessed by recently separated parents, to counsel children regarding their changed situation. Children can be dramatically affected by the actions of their parents. Children and parents have both reported that it has been beneficial to have counselling available for children, so that they can have a forum to discuss issues troubling them. I have also been able to assist children to present their point of view to parents and have that point of view heard by parents. This counselling and advocacy function which professionals can perform for children is seldom freely available. Yet parents who have separated are often in difficult economic circumstances and are unlikely to be able to afford professional fees. Public funding is available for counselling adults during separation and divorce. I believe this is highly appropriate. Often this counselling benefits adults and following this, there is a flow-on positive effect on children. **However, there is no public funding for counselling children during family breakups.** This seems to be a regrettable oversight given the frequent and far-reaching adverse effects on children of family breakups, and given the fact that children's best interests are viewed as paramount during Family Court proceedings. **I believe that a counselling service for children whose parents are in dispute regarding custody and access, would be a desirable addition to the services currently provided by the Family Court.**

Finally, I wish to discuss the concepts of custody and access which seem to be embedded in family law and in the minds of parents in New Zealand. I believe that these concepts have outlived their usefulness. Under New Zealand family law guardianship is the most important position with respect to influencing the upbringing of a child. If parents are married, both automatically become guardians of their children. Custody is conceptualised as the responsibility for the day to day care of the child. However, often parents approach Family Court proceedings with the view that custody is the paramount consideration. Having the Court confer the status of custodial parent on the mother or father, seems to be viewed as that parent having 'won' a dispute, with the 'access' parent being viewed as the loser. I believe such custody battles with the inevitable 'winners' and 'losers' can and should be avoided. We can help parents avoid drawing up battle lines by having a more sensible concept of what we are trying to achieve. Custody and access decisions are concerned with defining parental responsibilities in caring for their children in the future. My suggestion is that, rather than discussing and trying to reach decisions about custody and access, we should be assisting parents to form PACTs. PACT is an acronym for Parental Agreements to Continue to Care for Their Children. Each PACT formed between parents would define the mother and father's role in their children's life in the future. I believe that by encouraging parents to form PACTs, the emphasis on the process parents are engaged in, will be changed from a battleground to something hopefully representing a far more cooperative enterprise.

REFERENCES

Guba E. G. and Lincoln Y. S. (1981) *Effective Evaluation.* Jossey Bass Publishers, San Francisco

Patton M. Q. (1987) *How to use qualitative methods in evaluation.* Sage Publications Newbury Park, California

Panel Discussion –
Child, Parent and Family Support Services

Cathy Brown
Family Court Co-ordinator
Family Court, Dunedin

Co-ordination of the specialist services provided to the Family Court is the primary task of the Family Court Co-ordinator.

Specialist services include:

- counselling (conciliation)
- specialist reports on children
- counsel for child (lawyers to represent children)

In each of these areas, the Family Court Co-ordinator ensures that suitably qualified specialists are available to accept referrals or appointments and that they are adequately briefed as to what the Court requires of them.

This involves recruiting, selection, and ongoing training of these groups of specialists.

Family Court Co-ordinators liaise with all professionals involved in the Family Court such as Judges, lawyers, counsellors, report writers, social workers, community workers etc. They are also the public 'face' of the Family Court by answering inquiries from members of the public and talking to interested groups about the Family Court.

Catherine Goodyear
Director, Anglican Methodist Family Care Centre
Dunedin

I am the Director of an Agency which ten years ago, with six to eight workers, thought we knew what hard work meant. But in our current climate, our staff has grown to forty and we seem to work much harder, especially with the ever complex funding system which has evolved, to maintain our services.

Family Care has a range of services mostly based around supporting families. The theme of this seminar of supporting children and families through change is very much the philosophy of our Agency and most of our services have that focus. We do have services with a different focus, but they are not what this talk is about.

The services for families include:

- Counselling
- Budgeting
- Crisis Work
- Parenting Education Classes
- Homebuilders Family Support
- Caregiving Service
- Wide Horizons

I will speak in particular about these last three services.

It is not uncommon for a family to be involved in two or three of our services at any one time, with a 'seamless' and easy transition for those families to go from one to another.

However, I want to emphasise that when we look at family change, over the past few years, one Government policy change has been of huge significance to us and that was the benefit cuts of April 1991. In 1989 we gave out something like four hundred food parcels in that year to families. Last year we gave out three thousand, six hundred and eighty. The increase is significant for many reasons, but what I want to emphasise here is that as food bank numbers have risen, so have we seen a rise in family dysfunction.

We are not only working with the people who have an unhappy background, but who are also struggling to manage their lives on a day-to-day basis. No-one seems to be researching on an ongoing basis how the struggle to manage on that day-to-day basis is affecting the parents' energy levels and the resources they have for their children. It is now four years since the benefit cuts and we must not lose sight of the effects of these cuts. It is easy to forget and accept that this is the way things are.

So when we look at family change and services to help families, don't lose sight of the ecology in which a family lives.

Two of the three services I mentioned before have proved to be a way of working which have promoted considerable family change, and the third seems to have a marked effect on the well-being of some of the children who go through it.

1. Homebuilders Family Support

This scheme has been in existence in our Agency since 1982 and is a service offered to families who are experiencing difficulties managing areas of their lives, particularly with parenting and child behaviour problems. We have workers in Dunedin, South Otago, East Otago and Central Otago who have ongoing training through the Agency and come from a background of understanding children and family life. Workers have qualifications which include social work degrees, teacher training and play centre. But above all, they are chosen because they are parents and have an ability to relate on a very practical level with our client group. They work in the homes over a period of months and help the family set goals for the changes the family themselves wish to make. A Co-ordinator assesses the situation at the time of referral. At three months, they re-assess the situation, look at the changes that have been made, and together with the family, set goals for the next three months.

The changes that the family wants to make seem very minimal, but they are immensely important to the family. They have ranged from having the confidence to go down to the letter box to get the mail, or going off to University to get a degree. We have had experience of people who have achieved both these goals. The workers go into the home two, three, four or even five times a week, depending on the severity of the situation. Sometimes the situation is the result of a major crisis such as child abuse, but we also try to work in the area of prevention and education about parenting. One of the really nice things is when people come to us themselves and say 'Things are coming unstuck. You helped my friend along the road. Would you please be able to help me?' That situation is much easier to work with than referrals where families are directed to come because of abuse or some major crisis. The workers interact mostly with the parents, but they also sit and play with the children and help the parents to see other ways of understanding their children's behaviour and modelling positive interactions.

2. Caregiving Services

We are able to provide respite short term care for community referrals. This service is often used when families are in the process of some change as a preventative measure. This service's social workers and family support workers work together with a number of families and this easy co-operation in one agency appears to have a degree of success in helping families maintain positive change. Respite care is part of a plan which can greatly help relieve stress for parents and can assist them to get some energy to make the changes necessary in their lives.

3. Wide Horizons

Sometimes the children of families involved in other services are also involved in Wide Horizons, a children's recreation programme run in liaison with some of the schools in Dunedin. This programme provides outdoor experience and challenges for children who are showing signs of dysfunction in their homes and at school.

One of the important aspects about working with families through change is that you have to hear the parents and work with what they see are the problems. It is no use going into a family and saying 'There has been abuse', 'Your referrer has told us you can't manage the children', 'Wash the floor' or 'Do the dishes', etc. If the family see the problem as something different, that is basically where you have to start. So we have to look at providing social support as well as emotional support for the people who are trying to make changes in their lives.

If you look at the relationship between the adults and how that affects the children, it is very often professionals who will say 'These parents or this couple are fighting so much and that is what is making the kids behave like that.' If the parent sees the child as wicked or bad, that is where we have to start and it may take quite a long time before the parents can change their views and accept they have some responsibility to make appropriate changes. We are talking about giving power to parents and letting them direct the speed of change.

I wish I could say it all works beautifully, but it doesn't always. Mostly when our workers reach the end of what they can do, there have been some changes achieved. The evaluation sheets the parents fill in sometimes have an emotional effect on us and we feel very humble when we read things such as 'If it wasn't for your help, I would be over the edge of a cliff, because that's what I was going to do.'

As part of preparing for this talk, I consulted our workers and we discussed the issues that we see now compared to, say, five years ago. We also looked at our statistics. Child behaviour and child/parent relationships dominated our intake forms. These categories are what parents describe when they do the assessment sheets. Loneliness and isolation come very high, particularly for single parents. But the workers themselves say that particularly in the last two or three years, child violence is the issue they see more of now, especially from boys to their mothers, and the children can be very small, four or five years old, sometimes older.

It is important to remember that we need to give parents who are experiencing difficulties and going through change, a place in the world to help them gain confidence, we must really listen to what they are saying and help them with their own changes, rather than the changes we think they need to make.

Liz Price
Counsellor/Family Therapist
Logan Park High School

My role at school is one of advocacy. As the Counsellor, my main task is to help adolescents understand their own process more fully. I also work to resolve conflict in families and conflict between staff and students. The lynch pin in our guidance network at Logan Park is the group teacher. Most teachers are group teachers. We meet with the same group of students daily for the four or five years those students are at school with us. The older students are encouraged to care for the younger ones and the group teacher has ongoing contact with families.

Adolescence is of its nature, a transitional time. The messages given out by body piercing, different dyed hair and undergarments worn on the outside of clothing are all saying 'Honour me as a unique individual'. And often when they are acknowledged, adolescents need to blend in with their peers. In families, adolescents go into continuous negotiations about space and distance. They want to explore and take risks. Parents want to keep them safe. Parents need to protect their children who are trying to be independent in ways that are dangerous. Adolescents are under great social pressure to abandon their families, to be accepted by the peer group and to be autonomous individuals. Picking fights is a way adolescents have of staying close and maintaining distance at the same time, and can cause much confusion in their families. Some of adolescents' behaviour is not what parents think. The surface behaviour is not all there is. The deeper meaning is a quest for autonomy. As parents, we need to understand that distancing and hostility are not personal. I do acknowledge that understanding doesn't take the parental stresses away. It is difficult to be a loving, consistent parent in the face of stormy, explosive responses to such innocent questions as 'How was your day?' Parents sometimes assume that adolescents live in a world similar to theirs. They're wrong. Adolescents now live in a media-drenched world, flooded with visual images. It may be my age, but I welcome back the Beatles, all three of them, as positive models, as opposed to much of the rap, heavy metal currently involved, which is often very nihilistic, very negative and extremely anti-women.

Separation and divorce is a great shock to adolescents and they need to know parental separation is never their fault. A great number of my students whose parents separate, think and internalise feelings like 'If only I had kept my bedroom tidy'. As therapists, we need to be very clear that for whatever reason parents separate, it's not their children's fault and they have the right to be able to be age appropriate and grieve. It is very difficult.

Adolescence is a time when children are supposed to move away from their families, while the parents are firm and consistent behind them. Divorce disturbs this process. When the parents disconnect, the child feels outraged and abandoned, and even more so, if she or he is adopted because of the primal wound already incurred. When divorce occurs, we can help by creating space and having the time, as therapists, to hear and validate adolescents in their pain, outrage and hurt. Adequately funded, appropriately trained therapists can aid adolescents to navigate the trauma and depression that divorce can have.

When I was overseas, we went to Boston. There were eight Counsellors in a school in Boston the size of Logan Park. There is only one Counsellor for students at Logan Park High School and we don't have Counsellors in all our schools. We have some Guidance Teachers and a supportive guidance system. There is a huge range all over the world of therapeutic input.

We, as Therapists, Lawyers, Social Workers, need to speak out about liquor advertising, about insidious things like the nappy advertising that has babies with adult voice-overs. That's very nasty stuff. Anne Geddes calendars come into the same category. If we really think about it, what is the message in these advertisements?

The government has to assume the role of the good-enough parent.

Winnicott, the British Psychoanalyst, talked eloquently about most of us striving and achieving 'being good-enough parents'. But the government needs to take on this role by providing education for its politicians on understanding the process of childhood, by adequately funding caregivers and providing them with regular supervision and by acknowledging children as our greatest resource. Maria Warner, who is an author from England, wrote an essay called 'Fletcher's Families' and I quote 'I believe in children's rights to their childhood and childhood means freedom from pain, from coercion, from violence; the enjoyment of confidence, security and safety; access to food, to shelter and developmental skills. Much has been done over the last ten years to make life hard for parents and everything that makes life hard for parents, makes it hard on the children. In the era of the market force, children are suffering and with them, all of us are damaged.' Understanding the child's process and honouring children as the heart of our society is the answer.

When I was asked to write this, I talked to my seventeen-year-old son about what I should say. He said tell them 'Adolescents are lovely.' So, adolescents are lovely, and transitional, and very vulnerable.

Liz Price finished by reading 'Japonica', a poem from the Virago Book of Women Poets.

Marion Pybus
Department of Nursing and Midwifery
Massey University

The Contribution Of Public Health Nurses

I want to begin by reminding you of what you already know, that if a person hurts, they hurt all over. This is especially the case for children. Children hurt all over when they are hurt emotionally, and the help they are offered needs to reflect this holism.

While there is limited, but growing evidence of this holism (e.g. Marmot and Mustard, 1994) I would like to illustrate this holism using an indepth descriptive study I completed recently of the work of three public health nurses with fifteen families with children that were chosen because they were particularly stressed (Pybus, 1993). Family violence and/or alcoholism was evident in 11 of the 15 families, while being a sole parent was a major source of stress for the remaining four families.

When I came to describe the families, I found that in only one family where there was more than one child did all the children have the same father. In 12 families there was no adult male living openly at the address. Thus, separation and dissolution were relatively normal experiences for these families, with some evidence of custody, access and step-parenting issues.

When I examined the public health nurses' records of the 23 babies born into these families, I looked for evidence of chronic illness, and found the following situations:

Of the 23 babies,

- 8 were described as being premature
- 13 have records which show a pattern of regular upper respiratory infections and conditions, including 8 with asthma
- 6 are recorded as having recurrent ear infections
- 2 had gastroenteritis
- 3 had an inguinal hernia, one had a cleft palate
- 4 had recurrent eczema
- 3 had poor muscle tone, one of these is presently being tested for an unusual form of muscular dystrophy
- 2 who died had their deaths recorded as sudden infant death syndrome, while a third child had a near miss

Of these babies, there was just one baby who had no persistent disease recorded on their chart, and this baby was born during the study period, being just two months of age at the end of data collection. This baby was already experiencing regular upper respiratory infections by the end of this time.

As an in-depth descriptive study, there was no attempt to show formally that there was an association between living in a stressed family and physical ill-health. However, the data are consistent with my initial observation, that if one hurts, one hurts all over. Children do not just get emotionally sick, they get physically sick as well. Thus, it is not surprising to find nurses involved when children are experiencing family change and upheaval.

When the mothers of the study families were asked how the nurses helped them and their family, although mention was made of help with physical illness, the major emphasis was very much on psychosocial support:

I go to her if I'm going to hit rock bottom. 24

I really need them when I've had a gutsful. I feel much better after (N) has been and I've had a good cry. 34

I need the nurse when the walls close in. 33

The (public) health nurse has been the most useful of the health services. Just counselling about health and everyday life. When you are down, they give you a lift that helps you get through the day. 15

As well as interviewing the mothers, I got the nurses to record what they did when they visited each of these fifteen families, giving them a blank form to complete. I then analysed and grouped their responses as follows:

Summary of Nurses' Descriptions of their Interactions	
Focus of Interaction	
Parent	416
Pre-school	203
School age	115
Grandparent	51
Young Adult	35
Aspect of Person Focused on	
Psychological	307
Illness/Functioning	226
Behaviour	223
Physical	69
Development	19
Family	
Interaction	246
Material	218
Informal Networks	181
Formal Services	
General	182
Health – General	355
PHNs – as support	431
– as intermediary	71

It was quite clear that the mothers of these families valued the input of the nurses into their troubled circumstances. Yet today there is just one nurse doing this work, where before there were three, and she is doing it because she is too contrary, too pig-headed and too senior to allow herself to be moved elsewhere. Where once there were about 480 nurses, the majority of whom had this work as their major emphasis, there are now, to my best knowledge, just a handful throughout New Zealand, who are employed to do this work. While many community-based nurses work within a holistic perspective to the best of their ability, the organisational structure does not assist such an emphasis.

Nurses such as the three whose work is described here, helped families from a position that focused on helping the families help the children. They had a very limited legal base from which to gain entrance to families. And this was not necessary, as their work was to avoid the need for legal intervention.

One reference I used when analysing the data for this study made the following statement:

The style of therapeutic social control found in a group reflects its major form of social solidarity.
Horwitz, 1984, p.219

What I see is a move away from preventing problems towards using the law to treat them, however early this intervention. I am concerned that the child presenting with a sore tummy may not be recognised as a plea for help by an emotionally troubled child who is hurting all over.

REFERENCES

Horwitz, A.V. (1984). Therapy and social solidarity. In D.J. Black (Ed) *Towards a general theory of social control*, Otlando, Florida: Academic Press.

Marmot, M.G. and Mustard, J.F. (1994). Coronary heart disease from a population perspective. In R.G. Evans, M.L. Barer, and T.R. Marmor (Eds) *Why are some people healthy and others not?: the determinants of health*, New York: A de Gruyter.

Pybus, M. (1993). *Public health nurses and families under stress: promoting children's health in complex situations*. Palmerston North, Department of Nursing Studies.

Kevin Thompson
Manager, Child Support Unit,
Inland Revenue Department

Role of Agency

- To administer the Child Support Act which involves the assessment and collection of child support. Collective rates old (<40 percent) versus new (75 percent+).

Principles

- Children have the right to expect financial support from their parents whether they are living with them or not.

- The community has an interest in ensuring that caregivers of children receive adequate income – a fair child support system will ensure this happens.

Objectives

- To recognise the importance of the welfare of children.
- Simple, consistent scheme.
- Improve equity between custodial and non-custodial parents.
- Ensure obligations for birth/adopted children are not extinguished by obligations to step-children.

Trends

- Historically.
- Sole parent families increased from 10 percent of the total number of families with children in 1975 to 25 percent in 1991.
- In 1991, 1 in 5 families was a sole parent family supported by a benefit.
- This represented a cost of $1.1 billion to society in 1993.
- These trends have tested the traditional responsibilities of parents where many liable parents have not continued to support their children following separation.
- Their responsibility has been taken up by the taxpayer.
- In contrast, the parent who continues to provide care for the children of a broken relationship carries a large responsibility – 85 percent of custodians in 1991 were women.
- Children can be caught up in a conflict which often follows parental separation, especially when there is a disagreement over access/custody.
- It is in the interests of children both materially and emotionally that the provision of financial support should be resolved quickly – CSA tries to ensure this.

Current Trends

- Over the last twelve months, there has been a one percent increase in the number of liable parents and custodial parents.
- Increase in the number of liable parents nationally that are paying voluntarily (70 percent).
- Customers (both custodial parents and liable parents) appear to be more accepting of the Act, i.e. better informed, liable parents more receptive to paying.
- Gradual decrease in the number of custodial parents who are on a benefit – last twelve months reduced by nearly 5 percent from 78 to 73 percent.
- Increase in the number of males who are custodial parents – particularly in shared custody arrangements.
- Change in social attitudes to providing realistic financial support for their children.
- Initial criticism was embroiled in the emotional trauma associated with relationship breakdowns and a strong reluctance of many liable parents to meet their obligations – this has largely gone, e.g. 500 objections in 1992, 50 in the last twelve months.

Concerns

- Still a small group of 'hard core' non-payers – approximately 5-10 percent:
  - frequently self employed
  - missing customers
  - overseas

- Agency is actively taking court action against 'hard core' customers:
  - charging orders (property/possessions)
  - Arrest Warrants for those leaving New Zealand
- Difficulty in getting the required level of financial support from some liable parents:
  - F Vs being completed
  - exercising all available powers under the Act, e.g. 154 deductions/examinations

Latest Developments

- Administrative review process.
- Customer complaint service.
- 0800 toll free number.
- Organisation Review – establishment of Invercargill Office.
- Major review of agency electronic systems.
- Review of Child Support Act – Judge Trapski:
  - at cabinet
  - e.g. passing on points to custodians
  - estimations
  - hardship
  - custodians income
  - minimum/maximum liability

Statistics

120,000	Liable parents
<u>122,000</u>	Custodial parents
240,000	Total liable parents/custodial parents (1/4 million)
270,000	Children
$414 m	Collected all years
$150 m	Collected each year
70 percent	Liable parents paying on time
30 percent	Child support paid to custodians
70 percent	Child support paid to state
$190 m	Outstanding child support

Mavis Turnbull
Frontline Social Worker
New Zealand Children and Young Persons Service

Child, Parent and Family Support Services

The Children, Young Persons and Their Families Act of 1989 was brought in to reform the law relating to children and young persons who are in need of care and protection or who offend against the law. In particular, it was to advance the well-being of families and the well-being of children and young persons as members of families, hapu and iwi, and family groups and provide assistance for that to happen, and to make provision for matters of concern to be resolved by family.

Notifications to the NZ Children and Young Persons Service continue to come in at a steady rate, but what is of concern is that they are growing in complexity and seriousness, and are very often second and third generation. Children as young as eight years old are beating up on parents or teachers or other children and sexualised behaviour is common in some of the pre-school aged notifications. It is easier to work with parents who seek help than it often is when the notifier is a person within the community. There are still too many people who observe concerns and do nothing about it. Sad to say, some are professional people.

From a worker's point of view, it would be wonderful to operate as proposed by the Act – that is, assist families to resolve their problems. Too often the child comes from a parental situation where there is:

(a) no extended family able to assist. The child has identified with x number of mother or father figure heads.

(b) the other parent, usually the father, is either unknown or has seldom, if ever, been involved.

(c) the family is so dysfunctional that they are unable to resolve their problems or work with help.

(d) the parents' own childhood abuse has never been resolved.

(e) there is an alarming number of children who have either one or both parents suffering from mental illness.

Every effort is made to assist families, but work is hampered by the depleting resources available. We need agencies, such as the wonderful work being done by Anglican Family Care, triplicated; units such as the old Karitane Unit for young mums – where they could live and learn to care for their infants before being transferred to independence; specialised units for difficult teenagers and units where, under guidance, they could be trained with oversight towards independence. There needs to be support for men who care for their children. I believe that there are wonderful people in the community who could act as surrogate mums, grandparents, etc. for young families who are isolated.

Removal of a child from his or her biological family has psychological implications for individual family members and the family system. Reunification no doubt also evokes adjustments and reactions from both parents and children. The transitions children experience when their parents separate and they move through the access regimes is not easy. But for children in care, and returning home from care, it is more difficult as they are involved in a triad situation having formed attachments to the foster family where they have been kept safer. When returning to the family, the adjustments and reactions may be particularly stressful if parents and children receive few community services and show little improvement in problem areas, while the children are in care. Many do want to retain their foster family.

Entry to care involves major transitions, even traumatic upheavals with all the disorientation, stress and adjustments associated with such moves. Yet the entry to care is rarely unexpected.

Where parents have entered into a temporary care agreement while problems are sorted out, the transitions are usually made easier by the co-operative process, except in respect of teenagers whose already evident problems are compounded even further by the rejection!

In contrast, where children come into care via court orders, the transitions can be more difficult for all concerned. The primary deciding factor is that the best interests of a child must be paramount. Yet no matter how abused some children are, they do not want to be separated from their parent, even if that person is an abuser – I must add though that there are some children who fear any contact and actively avoid it.

Making a decision to return children must be carefully explored. At what point does frequent access between parents, family and child become return? When does lengthy absence from the home, as is common among adolescents, cease to be family membership? At what point do children cease to view their households as 'home'? What level of structural change in the natural family renders the transition *not* 'a return'? Is the family to which the child returns a 'site' or a set of relationships? The answers to these questions will differ according to the age, gender, class, ethnicity and culture of the family.

It is clear that the aftermath of severe difficulties at home can take many years to overcome. For the adolescent who returns home to a situation where the parent has difficulty in supporting them emotionally and financially, there is likely to be breakdown. These young people have a poor capacity to make effective lasting relationships and, in turn, this affects their ability to get a job or to stay in employment. They are reluctant to engage in further education or training and sad to say, are very difficult to find placements for. This is where a therapeutic living environment for this type of young person would be useful, where they did not have to interact like a family as in foster care. To say that, takes me to the subject of finance, which is what is required to provide the services children, young persons and their families require. Like other Government agencies what happens, or does not happen, is fiscally driven. Counselling is costly and there are insufficient funds available to provide for children's needs for counselling.

The final matter that concerns me in a Service such as ours that is fiscally driven is that there is no accountability in terms of child support paid by parents of children who come in to state care. Why this double standard in New Zealand? Parents who separate can apply to the Inland Revenue Department for an assessment and the liable parent pays whether they like it or not. There are some parents who are literally dumping their responsibilities on the state and yet are not accountable as yet (although I believe a working party may be being implemented).

Being called to account would mean the difference between the ability to have the services that we currently have not. It would also mean the parents be more responsible in general.

> *'The world breaks everyone and some become strong at the broken places.'*
> Hemingway

I would like to add:

'Some never become strong.'

Seminar Workshops

Nicola J Taylor
Project and Research Manager
Children's Issues Centre

Workshops were held following presentation of all the keynote papers. Participants were randomly divided into interdisciplinary groups and asked to address the following:

- **Policy, Practice and Research Issues** in such areas as Family Law, Education, Health, Psychological Services, Social Welfare services (including Income Support, Family Support agencies and the Children and Young Persons Service).
  – What needs changing because it is not working?
  – What is working well and how can this be supported?
  – What has not been addressed but needs to be?
  – What is the group's specific recommendation(s)?

Each group then reported back at a plenary session. The following major issues and recommendations were discussed.

- **Counselling for Children** – Publicly funded counselling should be made available to children and adolescents at an early stage when their parents are facing separation and divorce proceedings. Currently the Family Court only provides counselling for adults. We need to look at the cost of **not** counselling children – today's children are tomorrow's parents.

- **Important Role of Schools and Early Childhood Centres** – programmes need to be developed for life-skills programmes and parenting programmes. Schools and Early Childhood Centres can foster life-skills, positive role-modelling, self-esteem and conflict resolution.

- **Impact of Government Policies on Children and Families** – poverty is of paramount concern and needs to be addressed. A competitive funding environment creates barriers that stop families being helped.

- **Service Provision** – co-ordination of services to children and families is required – an holistic approach which integrates Votes Health, Education, Welfare and Justice. A cohesive needs based approach would help overcome the current emphasis on fiscal priorities and the separation of services and funding between individual departments. We also need to ask whether there are enough resources for stressed families? Which services and resources work best?

- **Valuing Children** – children need to be highly valued throughout any transition process. Unheard voice of the child needs hearing. Children's views about access arrangements should be taken into account.

- **Parent education** – effective parent education strategies are required.

- **Child Advocacy** – a Child Advocacy Service should be implemented (possibly linked with the Office of the Commissioner for Children).

- **Property Division** – children's needs should be accorded greater priority in the division of property following parental separation.

- **Fathers** – fathers should be encouraged and supported to remain involved in parenting their children following separation and divorce.

- **Legal Terminology** – the terms 'custody' and 'access' should be changed to move away from the implications of possession of the child and win / lose situations.

- **Privacy Act** – communication between and information sharing amongst different agencies is constrained by the Privacy Act.

- **Research** – priority should be given to conducting research ascertaining children's points of view during family transitions; research which focuses on family strengths and coping mechanisms was supported; studies which investigate the link between stress and health status should be undertaken; programme evaluation is important to highlight which services and resources are most effective for children and families experiencing family change.

- **Role of the Children's Issues Centre** – to raise the profile of children and parenting in society; to conduct research which can be used to better inform policy makers and politicians; to act as a catalyst; to facilitate networking; to offer regular seminars and conferences.

- **Multidisciplinary Co-operation** – need for multidisciplinary co-operation, in partnership with children and parents, in developing relevant research and policy on family transitions issues.

Summing up and Closing Remarks

Associate Professor David Swain
Pro-Vice-Chancellor, University of Waikato

Yesterday Judge Pat Mahony summarised very well what was presented and shared with us.

My focus is on several significant elements.

1 Useful data and findings known to social scientists and appreciated by practitioners.

Pool (1995) – quantity and perceived quality of reproduction and of parenting resources, and economic resources available to families.

Christchurch Child Development Study predictors of marital/family breakdown.

2 Government, politicians, journalists, commentators, etc don't seem to be aware of the available data/findings, don't listen when told.

3 There is little or no qualitative research on the subjective and influential understandings and meanings of family change for those experiencing it. Why?

4 Children's voices are almost entirely absent from research and policy debate, and limited in the Family Court process? Why?

5 There are gaps between what experts know and what practitioners know, and between what experts and practitioners know and what politicians and policy-shapers know. Why?

6 Public opinion is ill-informed and variable? But, when needs and problems are understood, New Zealanders are generous and caring, eg. Eve van Grafhorst and Telethon contributions per capita.

7 We have some reasons for cautious optimism or hope, yet the tone of public debate and the media is very pessimistic. Why?

8 We are obviously a highly creative society with innovative legislation and pilot projects and the ability to identify applicable overseas initiatives and adapt them to New Zealand . . . yet

9 . . . implementation often falters, eg. resourcing of family group conferences and their plans.

10 Even in accountants' terms, investment in prevention is worthwhile, i.e. the focus of the Children's Issues Centre's July 1996 conference.

11 There is wide acknowledgement of prevention being qualitatively better than cure . . . yet

12 There are almost no resources for prevention (and resources for expensive cures are being cut). Tax cuts before resourcing of good effective solutions (debt repayments OK).

13 Are we missing something here?

14 In Finland University, the Department of Social Policy is more accurately translated as the Department of Social *Politics*.

15 University of Waikato departments are *not* represented here, e.g. Department of Political Science and Public Policy – in which a former *politician* who was very successful in achieving policy and law changes lectured on *public policy*.

16 The only available case study of social legislation is of the Children, Young Persons and Their Families Act, 1989 – shows how complex and political the policy formulation process is.

17 Maybe some of the puzzles:
    – useful ignorance of politicians and journalists
    – lack of quality research on meanings
    – absence of children's voices
    – indifference to prevention
    – failure to follow-through on resourcing
    can be explained by the distaste of social scientists and practitioners for, and their lack of skills in, the politics of social policy formulation and legislation.

18 Maybe being right isn't enough? Maybe suggestions are not as effective as informed advocacy.

    Liz Price: 'Speak out . . .' Yes. In a politically astute way!

    There is a general election coming – our first MMP election – and it will be **THE** watershed. What are social scientists and social service practitioners going to do to influence its agenda and outcome?